For Kevin, Millie and Pippa

Contents

Introduction by Mick Waters

When I was a head teacher, assembly was such a significant part of the school. It was that chance to bring together all pupils to recognise, celebrate, acknowledge, think and enjoy each other's company. So it was with staff too, and assembly provided a way to talk with staff through the pupils. I think they call it modelling nowadays but, by showing how young people could be intrigued, fascinated, delighted, engrossed and thoughtful, we had food for thought about what should happen in classrooms and other teaching arenas.

I recall a series of weekly assemblies where the focus of attention was 'The Amaryllis'. How to drain every ounce from a simple idea! Week one in January saw the amaryllis removed from its box and placed in a pot by a group of children as the others were asked to think about promise and hope. The rather ugly looking corm would surely not attain the beauty of the illustration on the box. Only if we cared.

Week two saw the amaryllis pot at the front of the hall hidden inside a tall cardboard tube. Individual youngsters were invited to mark on the tube where they thought the amaryllis had reached in its growth. Because the tube was tall most estimates were high, so when the tube was removed the disappointment was palpable. There were no signs of growth at all. The accompanying homily referred to the amount of work going on inside, not yet showing; growth is happening, but currently without any discernible progress. The quest for instant results might be too demanding and we can't always see what is happening … albeit the same for children's learning.

As the weeks went by, we watched the stalk emerge and discussed support as a sensible precaution. The bud appeared and we talked about budding authors, artists, linguists and scientists, ready to make their impact.

At last we had the bloom. We were so pleased with it that we didn't even compare it with the picture on the box. It was so lovely in its own right. We had helped the plant to do its work with a little attention at the right time and we were able to celebrate its achievement, which was natural anyway. Then we discussed beauty and what it meant as a concept.

Then the bloom faded and we looked at the withering petals and talked about aging and renewal. All that from one flower!

Julie Warburton's book brings us into contact with an abundance of flowers and so many ideas of what they can do for all of us, children and adults alike.

I am pleased to introduce Julie and *Teaching with flowers for a blooming curriculum* in the hope that it will enrich children's lives. You will find the book is cleverly planned and written. The busy teacher will find instructions for arrangements that can be produced by children. There are step-by-step guidelines to help you take the children through the process of producing stunning flower arrangements. The photos will help you or the classroom assistant to structure practical sessions, and there are succinct tips on how to ensure success. Julie knows these arrangements work because she has created them all with children in schools as part of her blooming curriculum programme. I have heard adults gasp at what their pupils have produced and seen the delighted looks on children's faces as they achieve something of which they are rightly proud. Working with flowers has a profound effect on children.

Julie has much experience as a teacher and this comes through in her explanation of how to run the flower arrangement sessions. It also shines through in the sections where she explores curriculum ideas to sit alongside the practical flower arrangements.

The 'Let's learn about …' section is superb: Julie works through flowers to help you to teach aspects of many subject disciplines. The programmes of study teach three things: first, there are 'learning how to …' activities, using equipment and applying techniques. Next comes 'learning about …' where we build knowledge and understanding. Then there is 'learning through …' where one discipline supports or opens doors to another. If you feel trapped in a world of printed sheets and websites, this is a way to bring learning alive.

The history, science, art, geography and PSHE aspects of the work are given emphasis by the focus on flowers. Through flowers pupils are encouraged to think about the horrors of world wars and the science of propagation, medicine and colour. This links directly to the work of great artists and the use of flowers to create mood, including celebration. There are many uses of beautiful children's literature as a source of stimulus or extension, and the carefully researched references to sources of evidence, materials and stimulus for learning show the depth of Julie's teaching. The suggestions for homework, or 'learning to go', reinforce the demanding nature of the teaching. Working with flowers is not a soft option; school and learning should be demanding.

Julie has gone to great effort to offer advice on how to use flowers in other aspects of school life, and to show, how ideas fit together, how to resource the work you want to do and how to involve parents. She makes it all feel possible.

And it is. When you read what Julie has to say about how flowers affect people, you will see why this set of suggestions will make a difference to those children you teach. It will help to turn RAISEonline green but, more importantly, it will help to turn the children you teach into the sort of people you and their parents want them to be.

Enjoy watching the children you teach bloom with flowers.

The seeds of a blooming curriculum

You have probably picked up this book because you are looking for another way to help children learn, or perhaps you want to try something different, or maybe you love flowers and are intrigued about how you could teach many aspects of the curriculum through such an enchanting medium, or maybe it's a mix of all these things. Whatever your reason, and hopefully you are now reading your own copy, your pupils will thank you for it.

Teaching with flowers for a blooming curriculum has grown out of my own experience. I had been a teacher for many years, as well as a transition and literacy consultant, when I was given the chance to retrain as a florist. I then thought, 'What now?' There seemed to be a natural affinity between the two worlds, with the opportunity to use flowers to open the doors of the curriculum to children, so I decided to put together my knowledge of flowers and teaching. The blooming curriculum was born.

Initially, I was invited to work in schools to give children the experience of flower arranging and, to prevent it being a one-off event, I made links to what they were doing in many of the subjects across the curriculum. Gradually things became more structured, and the suggestions in this book come from the work I've done with children in classrooms and schools to help their curriculum bloom.

Teachers find that children's understanding of quite complex knowledge becomes much clearer when they take part in practical workshops. Most noticeable is the way that vocabulary is used by pupils as they explain their work. Teachers also tell me that they are impressed with the way children work in teams and that poor behaviour is rarely an issue. Even the most 'difficult' pupil seems to behave gently when given a delicate flower to work with.

I thoroughly enjoy doing workshops with children, teachers and parents, and the pride in the finished product is matched with the satisfaction of seeing learning taking place while people are at work.

This book is aimed at those who teach children aged 9 to 12 years. It offers an approach into an exciting and hands-on way of learning that captures children's imaginations by working with flowers, the most beautiful of natural materials.

Part 1
Just for teachers

Why you should use *Teaching with flowers for a blooming curriculum* in your classroom

There are many reasons why you should use this book and begin teaching with flowers. I'm going to list a number of them below.

Children love flowers. Flowers cheer them up and make them smile. Children get excited when they see flowers which means they are already hooked into what comes next. They are amazed and fascinated by the colour, shape, feel and scent of flowers. They will do anything for you to get a look at flowers. They bring in their friends from other classes to take a look at what they are doing. It's special. They know this. They can't wait to take to take their arrangement home. They want to do it again.

Staff love flowers. Flowers cheer them up and make them smile. Staff get excited when they see flowers which means are already hooked into what they are going to teach next. They are beguiled by the smell of flowers, as are the many visitors who pop in when word gets around that you have flowers in your classroom. Upbeat discussions begin containing the word 'love'. Staff want to do their own arrangement and take the flowers home.

Parents, relatives and guardians love flowers. Flowers cheer them up and make them smile. They are extremely pleased and proud of the wonderful floral arrangements made by their child. Children feel confident enough to go home and show their parents the new techniques they have acquired. Flowers are a wonderful way to draw in the crowds to your school – a school flower show can be a big hit, and

I encourage you to hold one at least once a year. Invite parents to help out, they love it!

When children get to handle, understand and appreciate real flowers, they begin to treasure their beauty and necessity in our lives. For some children this will be their first hands-on experience of working with real flowers and, with this in mind, I advise you to take great care in choosing beautiful, stunning or unusual blooms for the children to work with. Go to a flower wholesaler or market rather than the supermarket – the choice is far superior.

Working with flowers helps children to cover elements of the school and national curriculum in an imaginative, innovative and memorable way. Included in this book are helpful diagrams (see pages 14–17) that demonstrate which subjects, skills and elements of the curriculum are covered in each floral design and 'Let's learn about …' session. In this way, you can easily slot the lesson ideas and arrangements into your school's curriculum and your lesson plans.

You will cover a wealth of technical vocabulary including: angles, estimation, proportion, fractions, measurement, length, height, weight, gradation, number, cost, division, multiplication, subtraction, addition, perspective, colour, harmony, contrast, texture, form, line, space, balance, assembly, tools, production, structure, stability, strength, approximation, diagonals, invention, precision, surface area, botany, photosynthesis, stems, stomata, petals, sepals, roots, nectaries, stamens, carpels, pollination, growth, seeds, transpiration, habitat, environment, adaptation, weather, soil, landscapes, rivers, streams, mountains, grassland, woodland,

seashores … and more. You will also use lots of adjectives to describe the beauty of flowers.

Working with flowers is challenging yet achievable. All children will be able to do the arrangements and each one will be different from all the others in some way. Some of the techniques in the arrangements will be a challenge for them – although, amazingly, getting children to cut and apply sticky tape seems to be the biggest test! However, because they become so absorbed in what they are doing, they persevere, they help one another and they succeed. I have never, ever seen a child not be successful.

By working with natural materials, children will acquire new skills that are linked to real life. They will also see the practical application of academic subjects and topics; for once, understanding angles becomes relevant rather than a purely academic exercise.

Flowers give children and teachers a chance to be involved in a unique approach to learning. Without a doubt, you will all enjoy it and, when you enjoy something, learning becomes more natural and sparks the desire to learn more.

Working with flowers makes children feel good and boosts their self-esteem. They will all feel an enormous sense of achievement as there are no preconceived ideas or 'levels'. One 11-year-old boy once told me, after making a flower badge, that it was the best piece of art he had ever done. He evaluated himself without any prompting from me and without any reference to what level his work was at (and by cruel association, what level he regarded himself at as a person). I didn't even label the lesson as 'art'. We simply had a lovely, natural discussion about his opinions and experiences – and about flowers, floristry and the business of floristry. He left with a sense of achievement, quietly feeling very good about himself.

Despite the stereotypes, boys love learning with flowers, and staff have often commented how astonished they are by their level of absorption.

Without a doubt, teaching with flowers has a positive effect on the behaviour of children. Many teachers have been stunned by the significantly improved behaviour and motivation shown by their class demons and, interestingly, it is often these same children I identify as being the most helpful, eager to please and willing to share. Perhaps it is because teaching with flowers has purpose, momentum, offers something different, lacks routine, is exciting and new, uses wonderful materials and rewards and encourages

the development of practical skills alongside intellectual skills, or maybe it's because I have no preconceived ideas about the children I meet. This would make for some brilliant research!

In summary, teaching with flowers is imaginative, challenging, relevant, creative, educational, engaging, artistic, absorbing, calming, practical, worthwhile, inspiring, fun and memorable.

Chapter 2

Teaching with flowers and the national curriculum

When teaching with flowers, teachers need to know that they are addressing the content of the national curriculum in their lesson plans. It is rare to find floristry as a traditional subject discipline. Nevertheless, working with flowers is a wonderful vehicle for much of the directed content that children are required to study. The challenge for teachers is to find imaginative ways to bring alive the subject matter prescribed in the programmes of study. This is where floristry and flowers create wonderful learning journeys or inroads into subjects and, along the way, children will become more motivated and proficient.

So, to help you feel a little more secure about national curriculum delivery, I have plotted references against each 'Let's learn about …' activity in Chapter 8.

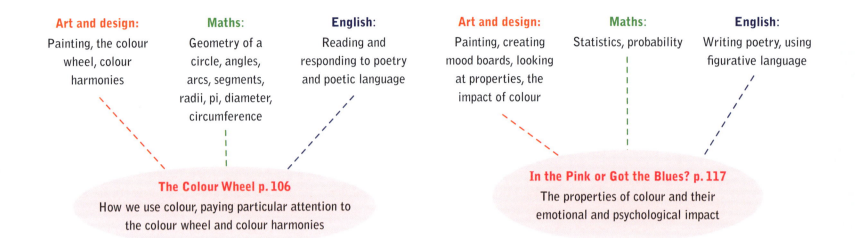

Art and design:
Painting, the colour wheel, colour harmonies

Maths:
Geometry of a circle, angles, arcs, segments, radii, pi, diameter, circumference

English:
Reading and responding to poetry and poetic language

The Colour Wheel p. 106
How we use colour, paying particular attention to the colour wheel and colour harmonies

Art and design:
Painting, creating mood boards, looking at properties, the impact of colour

Maths:
Statistics, probability

English:
Writing poetry, using figurative language

In the Pink or Got the Blues? p. 117
The properties of colour and their emotional and psychological impact

Let's learn about ...

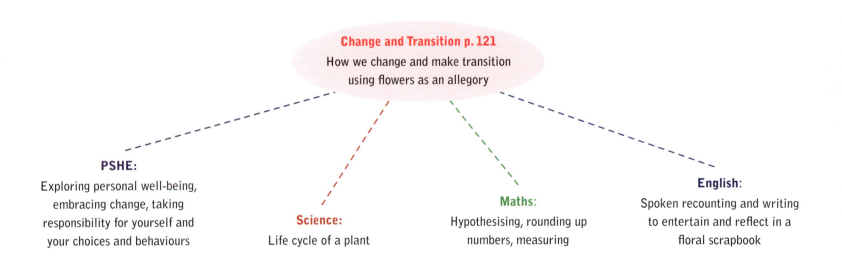

Change and Transition p. 121
How we change and make transition using flowers as an allegory

PSHE:
Exploring personal well-being, embracing change, taking responsibility for yourself and your choices and behaviours

Science:
Life cycle of a plant

Maths:
Hypothesising, rounding up numbers, measuring

English:
Spoken recounting and writing to entertain and reflect in a floral scrapbook

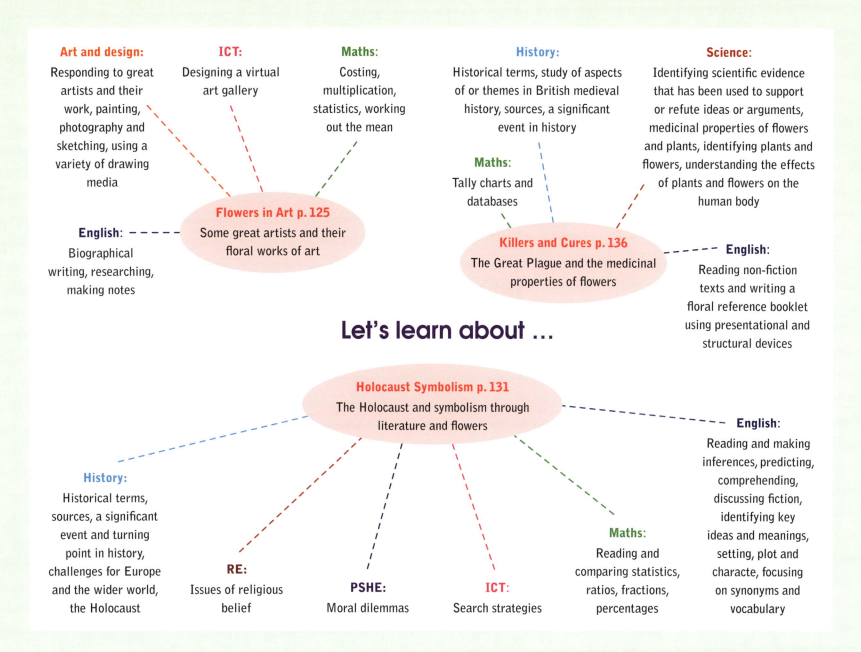

Art and design:
Responding to great artists and their work, painting, photography and sketching, using a variety of drawing media

ICT:
Designing a virtual art gallery

Maths:
Costing, multiplication, statistics, working out the mean

History:
Historical terms, study of aspects of or themes in British medieval history, sources, a significant event in history

Science:
Identifying scientific evidence that has been used to support or refute ideas or arguments, medicinal properties of flowers and plants, identifying plants and flowers, understanding the effects of plants and flowers on the human body

Maths:
Tally charts and databases

English:
Biographical writing, researching, making notes

Flowers in Art p. 125
Some great artists and their floral works of art

Killers and Cures p. 136
The Great Plague and the medicinal properties of flowers

English:
Reading non-fiction texts and writing a floral reference booklet using presentational and structural devices

Let's learn about ...

Holocaust Symbolism p. 131
The Holocaust and symbolism through literature and flowers

History:
Historical terms, sources, a significant event and turning point in history, challenges for Europe and the wider world, the Holocaust

RE:
Issues of religious belief

PSHE:
Moral dilemmas

ICT:
Search strategies

Maths:
Reading and comparing statistics, ratios, fractions, percentages

English:
Reading and making inferences, predicting, comprehending, discussing fiction, identifying key ideas and meanings, setting, plot and characte, focusing on synonyms and vocabulary

RE:
Global beliefs, ceremony, celebration

PE:
Dance, developing an understanding of dancing traditions, choreography and performing your own dance

Geography:
Locating countries on a map

MFL:
Spanish

Maths:
Fibonacci numbers, symmetry, 2D and 3D shapes

Music:
Listening, playing and performing, appreciating and understanding music from different traditions, improvising, composing

Let's Celebrate p. 140
The role flowers play in festivals, ceremonies and celebrations around the world

English:
Reading non-fiction texts and writing a flower language dictionary and folktale narrative

Let's learn about …

English:
Delivering a persuasive speech, making notes and writing a personal letter, reading and making inferences, predicting and comprehending, discussing fiction, identifying key ideas and meanings, setting, plot and character

Peace in Our Time p. 149
The after-effects of war and the organisations and charities that work towards peace. Look at the role flowers have played in brokering peace

Staying Alive p. 144
How a plant grows and reacts to conditions, including what this means for the florist

Science:
How plants grow, photosynthesis, transpiration, tropisms, applications of science

Maths:
Writing equations

English:
Reading non-fiction texts, delivering a speech as a fictional character, looking at prefixes and suffixes

History:
Historical terms, sources, a significant event and turning point in history, challenges for Europe and the wider world

Geography:
Locational knowledge, maps, human geography, population

Maths:
Understanding and presenting statistical data, mathematical reasoning, comparing, looking at value and rounding up numbers

Science:
Botany of a flower, pollination, reproduction

Maths:
Shapes, particularly triangles, acute and obtuse angles, measuring and working out circumference and area

English:
Role play, the etymology of words

Science:
Habitats, adaptation, classification, eco-systems

Geography:
Developing an understanding and awareness of physical geography using maps

Art:
Pictorial records, sketches, drawing maps

Where the Wild Things Are p. 161
Habitats around the world and in your local community

Maths:
Floral data collection

The Birds and the Bees p. 155
The botany of a flower and how it reproduces

English:
Reading fiction, writing a floral logbook and a plant hunter's diary

Let's learn about …

English:
Studying and using figurative language (e.g. alliteration, rhymes, puns, semantic fields, adjectives) and considering their impact on the reader, retrieving, recording and presenting non-fiction information, writing for audience and purpose, taking notes, writing to instruct for a magazine

A Career in Floristry p. 165
The business world of flowers and floristry

PSHE:
Exploring careers, information sources, enterprise and financial capability

Art and design:
Looking at floral designers, pattern, line, groupings

ICT:
Web page design

Maths:
Working out costings using addition, subtraction, multiplication, division, percentages and fractions

17

The following curriculum areas are also addressed in all 'Let's learn about ...' activities:

✿ English: spoken language – discuss, describe, relate, justify, ask questions, analyse, evaluate, interpret, express; reading – comprehension; writing – making notes.

✿ ICT: use of search technologies.

The following subjects are addressed through the flower arrangements. Learning will be developed through conversation and drawing pupils' attention to applications and processes studied in these subjects:

✿ Design and technology: design – generate, develop, model and communicate ideas through discussion; make, select from and use a range of tools and equipment to perform practical tasks accurately (e.g. cutting, shaping, joining, finishing); select from and use a wide range of materials and components, including construction materials, textiles and ingredients, according to their functional properties and aesthetic qualities; evaluate – assess their ideas and products against their own design criteria and consider the views of others to improve their work.

✿ Art and design: use, improve and develop art and design techniques.

Part 2
About flowers

Flowers are great – their colour, shape, scent and feel. I just love them and so do children. The only drawback to cut flowers is that once they have been removed from the main plant they are goners.

One way you can help your flowers look lovely for longer is to give them a little tender loving care on the day you purchase them, called 'care and conditioning' in the floristry trade.

Chapter 3
Care and conditioning for cut flowers

Fill your buckets with about 20 cm of water and add flower food if appropriate. Using your stem stripper or hands (this is my preference as it gives you more control and causes less damage to the stem – thorny roses are my only exception), remove any leaves that would sit below the water line so that around two-thirds of the stem is naked.

Cut the ends of each stem at a 45 degree angle (make sure you cut between the nodes on carnations as they will not be able to take up water if cut on the node). This widens the surface area of the stem and allows the flower to draw up more water. Place the flowers immediately into the water, taking care not to overcrowd them.

Keep the buckets in a cool, dark location until you are ready to use the flowers. I recommend you do this the day before you begin arranging as it will give the flowers plenty of time to hydrate.

These are the general care and conditioning requirements of flowers, but some are fussier than others. If in doubt, consult a florist, website or a book (*Cut Flowers: A Practical Guide to their Selection and Care* by Su Whale is easily available, as is the excellent reference book edited by Vanessa Gilbert, *Foliage for Florists*).

Some useful tips

To encourage flowers to open, place them in a light, warm place. You can add more water to your buckets, but make sure there are no leaves below the waterline.

Removing more leaves also encourages the buds to open as the water and nutrients are feeding the flowers rather than trying to support the leaves. Remove additional leaves if your flowers are looking particularly dehydrated. I tend to do this with chrysanthemums as they can spend a lot of time out of water before you buy them.

Keep your cut flowers away from fruits that produce ethylene gas, which some flowers are not very fond of.

Change the water every day until you are ready to use them in your arrangement. In this way, you avoid any bacterial growth that could affect the life of your flowers.

Chapter 4

The principles and elements of flowers and floral design

Before you embark on your wonderful floral journey, you might find it useful and interesting to understand some of the principles and elements of floristry. These should enhance rather than inhibit your creativity. Consider and experiment with these ideas, focus on one more than another or use them to talk about your final design.

Don't forget to pass on these nuggets of learning to the children!

Principles of design

Rhythm

Rhythm refers to the flow of the flowers within an arrangement, creating a sense of movement and encouraging the eye of the beholder to move around the design and linger. Rhythm is achieved by placement (lines, groupings and patterns); repetition of flower (focal, transitional, fillers), colour (tints, tones, shades and hues) or form (rounds, spears, spray/flat); and transition or gradation of flower size, colour or form.

Balance

There are two aspects to the principle of balance. The first is actual balance – will the finished arrangement be able to stand up on its own or has it been arranged with too much weight in one area so that it topples over? The second is visual balance – how pleasing and restful the design is to the eye. A design can be symmetrically or asymmetrically balanced and this is achieved through line, colour, use of space and weight of materials.

Proportion

Proportion deals with a ratio of one thing to another – it could be colour, texture, height or flower type. Florists take heed of both Euclid and Fibonacci when considering the ratio of one area to another in a floral design.

Euclid's golden ratio, in the simplest of terms, works in thirds – whether that is volume, area or line. For example, in terms of line, the total height of an arrangement should compromise one-third container, two-thirds tallest stems, or vice versa. Another example might be the use of texture within a design: one-third smooth, two-thirds rough.

Another method of measuring good floral design proportion is to adopt 3, 5, 8, part of Fibonacci's number sequence which, fascinatingly, reflects nature's very own growth pattern. So, using the above examples, your container to arrangement height ratio will be 3:5, or vice versa, making an overall number of 8. Rather than going for a line, you can use the Fibonacci sequence to group the flowers within your arrangement.

Contrast

Highlighting the differences in plant materials used in your design can add depth and dimension, drawing the eye to particular key areas. You can achieve contrast through colour, shape, size and texture. Be aware, however, that a contrast that is too strong or obvious may result in a loss of harmony and visual balance. It all depends on what effect you are trying to achieve.

Dominance

Dominance is when one element of the design is given importance – for example, the colour red may dominate or the round form of a tulip may take precedence over the line form of a genista. Dominance can be used to create focal points within your design.

Scale

Although often used in the same breath, scale and proportion are different. While proportion deals with a ratio quantity of one thing to another, scale deals with relative size dimensions. For the purposes of floral design, flowers can be divided into three sizes: focal, transitional and fillers (or big, medium and small if you like!).

Focal blooms are your big wow flowers or those with the most eye-catching, dominant colour. Peonies, roses, lilies, gerberas, standard carnations, standard chrysanthemums, dahlias, sunflowers, anemones and proteas are just some examples.

To bridge the gap between the big focal flowers and the tiny fillers, use transitional flowers, such as spray roses, spray chrysanthemums, spray carnations, eryngiums or ranunculi.

All good things come in small packages and filler flowers can be incredibly gorgeous. Some of my favourites include waxflowers, asters, hypericum, tanacetum, genista and kangaroo paw.

Think about the scale of one flower next to the other when creating your design – big to medium or medium to small will work much better than gigantic next to tiny.

Harmony

Harmony is the sum of all the above parts, resulting in a design where all the components work well together.

Elements of design

The elements of design feed into your principles of design.

Line

Lines are talked about a lot in floral design. They help to create the movement and rhythm of an arrangement, forming a path for the eye to move along – think patterns. You can place your flowers in a diagonal line, a horizontal line or a vertical line, as well as a lazy 'S' line, to attain your desired effect. More than one line in a design is also possible. You can create lines using one flower type or a group of flowers or by repeating colour.

Form

Form relates to the shape of your final design and the shape of the floral material used within the design. I will concentrate on the latter.

In simple terms, flower shapes can be divided into three major forms: rounds, sprays and spears. Try to include a mix of two or three of these shapes to add interest to your design. Nonetheless, some very effective and stunning designs rely on using only one form or flower type. Look at some floristry magazines and the internet for ideas (see Part 4 for some ideas to get you started).

Rounds

Rounds include domes, globes, flats and rosettes. The large round form flowers are generally used as the focal, or main, flower within a design. That is, they are the dominant flower that creates a centre of interest and allows the eye to rest and linger as it moves around the arrangement. Some rounds like alliums and craspedia look wonderful in modern, minimalistic designs.

Hydrangeas, roses, dahlias, peonies, tulips, gerberas, alliums, orchids, open lilies (when closed they are spears!) are some other rounds you could use.

Spray

Spray flowers have flowering branching stems away from the main stem. The flowers are smaller in size than 'standard' flowers – that is, flowers with only one main stem (like a gerbera). Spray flowers can be used as transitionals or fillers, depending on the size of the flowers. They can

soften a design, especially the lovely fluffy ones, and add variation and interest.

Spray flowers you could use include eryngiums, waxflowers, gypsophila, spray chrysanthemums, Michaelmas daisies, spray roses, *Alchemilla mollis* and statice.

Spears

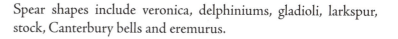

As you can tell by the name, these are your 'pointy' flower forms. They add direction, structure, form and height, and they contrast well with round forms. Spears can help to lead the eye from the outer edges of the design to the desired focal point. They are usually made up of lots of smaller flowers on short stalks (some are even stalkless) growing up to the tip. They generally flower from the bottom up, though there are a couple of exceptions (e.g. liatris) which flowers from the top down.

Spear shapes include veronica, delphiniums, gladioli, larkspur, stock, Canterbury bells and eremurus.

Texture

When evaluating a floral design, florists consider actual texture (how the floral material feels) and visual texture (how it looks). A shiny texture makes the eye move quickly over the design, while a rougher texture will halt the eye. This is because there are generally more gradients of colour lying within a textured flower which are enhanced by differences in light. A monochromatic colour scheme with differing textures can look stunning and intriguing, as the texture can add a wonderful three-dimensional aspect to your design as well making your arrangement irresistibly tactile. You may need to add a 'Please do not touch' sign to your design!

Colour

Colour is the diva of the elements of design! Nothing influences our moods or emotions like colour – it is usually the first aspect we respond to. Colours have symbolism, associations and connotations. They can clash, argue and fight, or they can be serene and harmonious. Whatever colour combination you choose, you will always get a response. I will cover colour in much more detail in Part 3.

Space

Space is probably the trickiest of the elements to describe and the hardest for students of floristry to get right. I could describe the concepts of positive and negative space but, without trying to get too complicated about it, basically make sure you allow for space within your design to give an illusion of depth. This will add interest and allow the eye to rest for a while.

Chapter 5

Making changes:
flower colour and seasonality

Although I have tried to use flowers that are available all year round (referred to as AYR by wholesalers), some flowers are seasonal. You may therefore need to make substitutions depending on what time of year you make your floral designs. Alternatively, you may want to make changes because you would prefer to use a seasonal bloom or a different flower or colour scheme.

Whatever the reason, to get you going I have provided a top ten chart so that you can cross-reference colour with seasonality. I have included focals, transitionals and fillers in each colour group, as well as a mix of flower shapes. All the flowers listed are readily available, but there are lots more lovely and spectacular ones out there. Develop a good relationship with your local flower seller and they will always be happy to advise, or consult one of the recommended books listed at the back of the book if you want to delve further.

Note: Roses, carnations, freesias, lilies, chrysanthemums, eustomia, alstroemeria and gerberas are available in most colours all year round.

Yellow	Spring	Summer	Autumn	Winter
Craspedia	✿	✿	✿	✿
Daffodil	✿			
Dahlia			✿	
Eremurus		✿		
Forsythia	✿			
Mimosa	✿			
Ornithogalum	✿			✿
Ranunculus	✿			✿
Sunflower		✿		
Tulip	✿			

Orange	Spring	Summer	Autumn	Winter
Alstroemeria	✿	✿	✿	✿
Asclepia	✿	✿	✿	✿
Carthamus		✿	✿	
Celosia		✿	✿	
Dahlia			✿	
Eremurus		✿		
Ornithogalum	✿			✿
Physalis			✿	
Ranunculus	✿			✿
Tulip	✿			

Red	Spring	Summer	Autumn	Winter
Amaranthus		✿	✿	
Anemone	✿			
Celosia	✿	✿	✿	
Crocosmia		✿	✿	
Gladiolus		✿	✿	
Heliconia	✿	✿	✿	✿
Hypericum (berry)	✿	✿	✿	✿
Peony	✿	✿		
Ranunculus	✿			✿
Tulip	✿			

Pink	Spring	Summer	Autumn	Winter
Alpinia		✿	✿	✿
Amaryllis				✿
Astilbe		✿	✿	
Consolida		✿	✿	
Gypsophila	✿	✿	✿	✿
Hyacinth	✿			✿
Peony	✿	✿		
Phlox	✿	✿	✿	✿
Stock	✿	✿		✿
Tulip	✿			

Purple	Spring	Summer	Autumn	Winter
Allium	✿	✿	✿	
Anemone	✿			✿
Aster	✿	✿	✿	✿
Callicarpa (berry)			✿	✿
Delphinium		✿	✿	
Hyacinth	✿			✿
Liatris	✿	✿	✿	✿
Limonium	✿	✿	✿	✿
Trachelium	✿	✿	✿	✿
Tulip	✿			

Blue	Spring	Summer	Autumn	Winter
Agapanthus	✿	✿	✿	✿
Ageratum	✿	✿	✿	
Campanula		✿		
Delphinium		✿	✿	
Eryngium	✿	✿	✿	✿
Hyacinth	✿			✿
Hydrangea		✿	✿	
Iris	✿	✿	✿	✿
Lavender		✿		
Scabious		✿	✿	

Green	Spring	Summer	Autumn	Winter
Alchemilla		✿		
Amaranthus		✿	✿	
Bupleurum		✿	✿	
Brassica		✿	✿	✿
Cymbidium	✿		✿	✿
Hellebore	✿			✿
Hydrangea		✿	✿	
Molucella	✿	✿	✿	✿
Ranunculus	✿			
Viburnum	✿			✿

White	Spring	Summer	Autumn	Winter
Aster	✿	✿	✿	✿
Astrantia		✿	✿	
Dendrobium	✿	✿	✿	✿
Eryngium	✿	✿	✿	✿
Genista	✿			✿
Ornithogalum	✿	✿	✿	✿
Snapdragon	✿	✿	✿	✿
Stock	✿	✿		✿
Veronica	✿	✿	✿	✿
Waxflower	✿	✿	✿	✿

Why not ask the children to find pictures of the flowers and identify which are focals, transitionals and fillers? They could also do a shape-sorting activity (classifying flowers into rounds, spears or sprays) and then use the photos as part of a display.

33

Moss

Mosses come in lots of interesting varieties, they are immensely textural and they can be used in many ways. Indeed, there are very few arrangements in this book that do not make use of moss in one way or another. The three mosses I have used in this book are readily available. They are:

❀ Sphagnum moss: This is damp and is sold in small sacks. It is great for covering floral foam on your finished arrangement.

❀ Spanish moss: This looks like pale green elastic bands and is sold in small boxes. It lends a very delicate and dignified rusticity to a design.

❀ Black moss: This is a crusty, brittle moss and is good glued on to designs as a dramatic base. It is used a lot in contemporary designs.

Part 3
Teaching with flowers

Chapter 6

Working with the blooming curriculum

Included in Part 3 are twelve flower arrangement ideas and twelve 'Let's learn about …' sessions for you to use with the children.

The arrangements cover a variety of professional floristry techniques for you to teach to the children and for them to become skilled in. The instructions are designed for the teacher, and I would advise you to have a go first before demonstrating these in front of the class. Each arrangement details what flowers and equipment you will need before taking you through the design using step-by-step instructions and helpful photographs. The expectation is that the children will then make their own wonderful arrangement to display at school or take home.

Each 'Let's learn about …' activity contains teaching and learning ideas, key vocabulary to use, subjects you might like to discuss, a 'Learning to go' homework activity and English and maths links called 'Extra English' and 'A fraction of maths'. I have deliberately not given any time indicators; it is for you to decide how far and at what pace you want to take the activities and ideas suggested.

Vocabulary

Along with the key vocabulary provided in each 'Let's learn about …' session, the arrangements themselves also offer opportunities for developing children's vocabulary. Listed below are a few pointers and key words you could include:

✿ Teach and use the Latin names of flowers which, in turn, will ultimately lead the children to a greater understanding of classification. The names can appear tricky, but children pick them up with no problem and actually enjoy using the correct terminology.

✿ Use botanical terms for flowers as you handle them (e.g. stem, petal, tepal, sepal, stamen, carpel, calyx, corolla) and discuss the causes and effects of, for example, transpiration and phototropism.

✿ Talk maths as you cut and place stems at angles, consider the surface area of cut stems, measure and estimate, think in proportions (generally thirds) and fractions, and achieve the correct balance by considering height, length, weight and placement of flowers in a design.

✿ Evaluate the design with vocabulary such as form, line, texture, colour, harmony, contrast, perspective, gradation, assembly and structure.

Linking the flower arrangements and 'Let's learn about …' sessions

Although each arrangement has been designed specifically to fit with one 'Let's learn about …' activity, many of the arrangements can be linked to more than one. These are detailed below with the main arrangement appearing in pink and related arrangements in green. At the end of each set of arrangement instructions, I have included some ideas and questions you could use with children to link the arrangements with the 'Let's learn about …' sessions, but feel free to find your own links too!

Flower Arrangements

Let's Learn About …	Nature's Colour Wheel p. 44	A Cottage Garden p. 48	Striking Strelitzia p. 52	Sunflowers p. 56	Six Yellow Flowers p. 60	Herbal Tussie-Mussie p. 64	Mask Your Feelings p. 70	Peace Wreath p. 74	Test Tubes p. 80	Woodland Wall Hanging p. 86	Fantasy Island p. 92	Fabulous Flower Badge p. 98
The Colour Wheel p. 106	✿	❀	❀	❀	❀	❀	❀	❀	❀	❀	❀	❀
In the Pink or Got the Blues? p. 117	❀	✿	❀	❀	❀	❀	❀	❀	❀	❀	❀	❀
Change and Transition p. 121	❀		✿							❀		
Flowers in Art p. 125			❀	✿						❀		
Holocaust Symbolism p. 131					✿							
Killers and Cures p. 136						✿						
Let's Celebrate p. 140							✿					
Peace in Our Time p. 144								✿				
Staying Alive p. 149									✿			
The Birds and the Bees p. 155										✿		
Where the Wild Things Are p. 161										❀	✿	
A Career in Floristry p. 165		❀		❀		❀		❀				✿

A few things to consider about the flower arrangements

I have given quantities, colours and named certain flowers for each of the arrangements, but you are welcome to substitute and to let the children pick and choose, leave things out, adapt or create their own designs – they are generally very good at this. I usually show them the techniques, explain the floristry principles, demonstrate and then let them get on with it.

It is best to demonstrate the arrangements in stages. I ask the children to gather around my demonstration table or get into a position where they can see what I am doing. I do a little and then they return to their workstations and have a go. I then regroup and show them the next stage, all the time keeping up a brisk pace.

Try to have another adult in the room if you are working with a group bigger than fifteen. That extra pair of hands is invaluable.

The 'What you need' section accompanying each of the flower arrangements lists the materials required for one child/arrangement. I have tried to make it as cost-effective as possible without losing too much impact. However, if you wish to push the boat out there are many weird, wonderful and amazingly beautiful alternatives – the only constraint is imagination and money!

I find having a flower-filled bucket per three or four children at a workstation works well, unless you have really fragile flowers that may get damaged, in which case, hand these out when the children are ready to use them in their arrangements. Although I have

never experienced it yet, be prepared for some little squabbles if child A nabs child B's flower because they've cut theirs too short.

Flowers and foliage come in groups of five, ten, twenty and twenty-five – for example, you can only buy gerberas in packs of twenty stems. This is something to think about when calculating amounts needed and cost. Brush up on your mental maths, if need be, as you will need a lot of it in floristry!

The arrangements should last for about a week. Water and mist the blooms regularly to help them last longer. If you neglect them, they will wither and die within a day or two.

Chapter 7
The flower arrangements

You will need:

Flowers and foliage

5 stems of red ranunculus

2 stems of green phlox

1 stem of orange ornithogalum

1 stem of blue delphinium

1 stem of mimosa (this can be shared between 2–3 children)

1 stem of purple limonium

A few generous handfuls of flexible twigs and twine, such as birch, spruce, honeysuckle, ivy or clematis

Equipment and sundries

Reel wire

30 cm wire wreath frame

Floristry glue

Floristry scissors

Nature's Colour Wheel

Learn how to bind and make a rustic colour wheel using nature as your palette.

✿ First, bind the twigs and twine to the wire frame to make a good solid base on which to glue your flowers. Do this by grabbing a generous handful of twigs and twine, placing this on top of the wire ring and binding with your reel wire. You only need to place the twigs and twine on one side of the wire ring. Keep repeating this action, going around the frame until your wreath is covered with the twigs and it looks a little bit like a bird's nest. Cut the wire and tuck in the end. Don't worry if bits of twig or twine stick out as it adds to the natural look of the wheel. To add further interest, leave some of the twine cascading away from the wheel as I have done.

✿ Now your base is ready you can think about the placement of the flowers on your wheel. It is best to cut and place all your flowers first before you glue. In this way, you can play with the pattern before committing yourself.

✿ Cut the flowers close to the calyx leaving only a little bit of stem – no more than a centimetre.

✿ When you are happy with your pattern, glue the flowers on by popping a small amount of floristry glue on to the back of each flower. You have now created your very own nature's colour wheel to give to a friend, family member or to keep for yourself!

Let's learn about links

✿ **The Colour Wheel:** As all the colours in the colour wheel exist in nature, instead of painting, ask the children to make a colour wheel from flowers instead. Alternatively, they could choose to go monochromatic and show a hue and its corresponding tints, tones and shades, or go for a vibrant polychromatic colour scheme.

✿ **In the Pink or Got the Blues?:** Discuss with the children which colours appear to recede and which colours appear nearest to them. How do the colours in their design make them feel?

✿ **Change and Transition:** How did the children make the transition between different colours a smooth one? How did the transition in size help to make the arrangement balanced?

You will need:

Flowers and foliage

1 or 2 long stems of willow, cornus or hazel

3 stems of pink tulip (peonies, gerberas and roses would also work well)

2 stems of blue delphinium

3 stems of astrantia

2 stems of bupleurum

1 stem of polygonatum

1 stem of trailing ivy

Handful of sphagnum moss

Birch bark

Equipment and sundries

Third of a block of floral foam plus any offcuts

Round container (e.g. a large yoghurt pot)

1 piece of raffia

Floristry scissors

Secateurs

Reel wire

A Cottage Garden

Bring a little bit of the garden indoors using blowsy and beautiful cottage garden favourites and learn how to make a simple trellis too!

❋ Soak your floral foam in water and place it in the centre of your container. If you have any offcuts then stuff these into any gaps.

❋ To complete the container, you will need two layers of birch bark cut into strips. The first layer of strips should be slightly taller than the container and the second layer slightly shorter. Glue the taller strips around the edges of the pot first. You will need some patience for this as it does take a little time for the glue to stick. Next, glue the short strips around the container. This gives a layered, rustic effect. Don't worry about any gaps or the pot being visible in places as you can cover this with moss later. Finally, tie a piece of raffia around the pot to secure the birch bark strips in place.

❀ Now make the trellis. You are aiming for a fan shape. Cut the long stem of willow so that you have three tall vertical sections and three horizontal sections, each slightly shorter in length but long enough to span the three vertical pieces of willow – a bit of measuring is advised. Place one tall vertical stem centrally in the rear third of the foam and the other two tall pieces on either side. Make sure these two pieces are placed at an angle in the foam to create the fan shape and that they are all in line with each other. Secure the three horizontal pieces of willow to the vertical pieces using reel wire to create a frame.

❀ You are now ready to insert the flowers. Insert the blue delphiniums first, one to the rear and right of the frame and the other, cut slightly shorter, in front of the frame and positioned in the middle. This creates a diagonal line for the eye to follow.

❀ Next insert the three focal flowers to create a triangle – secure them to the frame with a little reel wire if necessary. If you are using tulips, you can make them bigger by inverting the petals firmly, but with care – they become a completely different flower!

✿ To soften the lines a little, create two arc shapes with the ivy and polygonatum. Insert the ivy on the outer edge of the design and twine it around the climbing frame. Place the polygonatum closer to the centre and create an arc by binding it delicately to the frame at the top.

✿ Finally insert your fillers, the astrantia and bupleurum, and cover the floral foam and any gaps in the container with sphagnum moss. You now have your own cottage garden indoors – at any time of year!

Let's learn about links

✿ **The Colour Wheel**: Discuss with the children what kind of colour harmony is used here and consider where else they might see blue and pink together. Are hues, tints, tones or shades used? Ask them how different the arrangement would look if you had used just one colour.

✿ **In the Pink or Got the Blues?**: Ask the children what colours they normally associate with the colours pink and blue. How do they emotionally respond to each of the colours? Which colour appears warmer or cooler? Which colour appears nearer or further away?

✿ **A Career in Floristry**: Ask the children to describe the customer who would buy this arrangement. What advice would they give them to keep it in good condition?

Striking Strelitzia

An unusual yet striking contemporary arrangement that will not fail to impress (inspired by a Hans Haverkamp design).

❀ To make the container, soak the floral foam in water and place it centrally on the cellophane.

❀ Wrap the cellophane around the foam and secure with sticky tape. Cut away any excess.

❀ Next, glue one side of the jute strip and wrap it around the foam block.

❀ Now begin to insert the floral material into the foam (don't forget to cut all stems at a 45 degree angle). Start by inserting the five strelitzia leaves in a slight fan shape. These need to be left quite tall and placed in the rear third of the foam.

❀ Once you have done this, puncture the leaves with the Midelino sticks and thread them through the leaves – connecting at least two each time. Thread your pearls and paper petals on to the sticks in any pattern so that some are in-between the leaves and some are at the ends. Secure your pearls and petals in place using the tiniest amount of glue.

❀ After completing your strelitzia framework, you can start inserting the rest of the floral material. Place the two gerberas on the left-hand side and the two dianthus on the right-hand side of the design. Make sure they are of different heights (as in the photo). Insert each liatris and allium stem in-between the strelitzia leaves.

❀ Insert the two green hypericum stems low into the design and pop in the *Fatsia japonica* leaf next to the dianthus, ensuring it is inserted at a very acute angle to make it lie flat. Cover any exposed foam with moss.

✿ Finish off by decorating your container with a piece of raffia. Get ready to stun!

Let's learn about links

✿ **The Colour Wheel:** Ask the children to look at the colour harmonies within this design. What colour scheme is being used? What tints, tones, hues and shades are used?

✿ **In the Pink or Got the Blues?:** Discuss with the children how the colour scheme effects them emotionally. Does the choice of colours suggest a particular emotional purpose?

✿ **Change and Transition:** Ask the children to consider change and transition in the colour scheme, the transition of space (e.g. more space as the strelitzia leaves fan out) and change and transition in flower shape and size.

✿ **Flowers in Art:** This is a contemporary artistic design. Does it remind the children of any pictures or art styles they have seen or know about?

✿ **A Career in Floristry:** As this is quite an unusual and striking design, it would probably be suitable for a special event or corporate environment. What type of setting do the children think it might suit? Ask them to calculate the production and retail costs of the arrangement.

Sunflowers

Tall and stately, this arrangement is front-facing, contemporary and rustically sophisticated. A test in proportion and balance!

✿ To make the container, soak the floral foam in water and place it centrally on the cellophane, tall and slim.

✿ Wrap the cellophane around the foam and tape into place. Cut away any excess and, since you may end up with a lot of bulky cellophane, tape around the sides near the top to secure further.

✿ For this next step, I would recommend enlisting the help of a friend. Place the poplar bark around the cellophane-wrapped foam and ask a friend to secure it with twine while you hold the bark in place. Don't worry about any small, thin gaps between the bark as you can always fill this with sphagnum moss at the end. Tie another piece or two of twine around the bark container to ensure it is secure. Tie as tightly as you can – your friend might like to help hold the twine in place while you knot it.

✿ Now for the easy bit – arranging the flowers and foliage! Begin by arranging the grevillea leaves, aiming for a tall, elongated teardrop or isosceles triangle shape, with the tallest piece about twice the size of the container. Place the tallest piece centrally at the rear of the container followed by two slighter smaller pieces on either side, gradually diminishing in height until you have the desired outline shape. Fill in the foam with rest of the grevillea so it looks lush and fairly dense.

✿ Next, insert your three sunflowers into the base of the container – the first centrally and the other two placed on either side but angled slightly forward. Fill in-between the grevillea with the dried nigella and genista, although try to keep this fairly low and not too dense.

✿ Finally, fill any gaps in your container with sphagnum moss.

Let's learn about links

✿ **The Colour Wheel:** Look at the colour harmonies within this design. Ask the children to identify the colour scheme used and discuss how tints, tones, hues and shades are used.

✿ **In the Pink or Got the Blues?:** How does the colour scheme effect the children emotionally? Does the colour palette suggest a particular emotional purpose?

✿ **Flowers in Art:** This is a contemporary and artistic interpretation of van Gogh's life – it incorporates sunflowers from his famous series of paintings, while the grevillea leaves are inspired by *The Starry Night* and represent the unwieldy swirls of van Gogh's unstable mind. Get the children to take a photograph of their design and add it to their virtual gallery or display it along with other art-inspired flower arrangements.

✿ **A Career in Floristry:** As this is quite a sophisticated design, there is no reason why it couldn't be used as a display at a special school event. Who do the children think might buy this arrangement and for what occasion? What environment would it suit? How much would they sell it for? What school event might they create it for and where would they place it for maximum impact?

You will need:

Flowers and foliage

3 stems of bleached mitsumata (for a cheaper arrangement, substitute with a selection of tall twigs)
2 stems of bleached gypsophila
2 stems of salix (pussy willow)
1 stem of white *Lilium longiflorum*
2 stems of yellow tulip
2 stems of yellow gerbera
2 stems of yellow ranunculus
1 stem of white eryngium
2 stems of *Galax urceolata*
Handful of sphagnum moss

Equipment and sundries

1 strip of jute material (9 cm x 100 cm)
20 cm length of red ribbon
1 piece of black raffia
1 block of floral foam
Cellophane
Sticky tape
Floristry glue
Floristry scissors

Six Yellow Flowers

This is an austere yet very beautiful asymmetrical design using yellow flowers of varying shades.

❀ To make the container, soak the floral foam in water and place it centrally on the cellophane.

❀ Wrap and tape the cellophane around the foam. Cut away any excess.

❀ Next, glue one side of the jute strip and wrap this around the foam – with the glue side touching the foam, obviously! Then wrap the raffia quite tightly around the middle of the jute and knot or make a bow. Trim any excess. This gives your container a slightly more decorative effect, yet still retains an austere, serious feel.

Start by inserting the bleached mitsumata to create the feeling of a forest. Insert the mitsumata into the rear third of the foam, a couple of taller mitsumata at the sides and a few smaller ones in the middle to create a dip effect. This will allow the eye to move along the outline of your design and create a sense of space. Slightly stagger the line of the mitsumata too, with some a bit further back or forward than the others. This gives a more natural look as well as adding depth and interest to the design.

❀ Now begin to insert the floral material into the foam – don't forget to cut all stems at a 45 degree angle.

✿ Next, insert the pussy willow among the twigs, making sure that they are at slightly different heights. Again, this encourages the eye to travel through your design.

✿ Moving on to the flowers, insert the lily on the left-hand side of the design (as you are looking at it), among the twigs, ensuring that it is about two-thirds of the height of the twigs. Don't forget to measure before you cut – you can always cut more off, but you can't glue a bit of stem back on!

✿ Insert the six yellow flowers as they appear in the photograph, ensuring that they are cut to different heights and they are staggered along the front two-thirds of the floral foam. You are aiming for an asymmetrical shape.

✿ Cut off the shoot stems of the eryngium close to the main stem (this will provide you with more flowers) and insert these quite close to the floor of the floral foam. Add the two galax leaves, one in the front corner and one at the rear.

✿ Cover all the floral foam with moss, stuffing it in-between the flowers and mitsumata, but taking care not to damage any of the petals or stems.

✿ Finally, tie the red ribbon to the mitsumata on the right-hand side of the design to give a sense of balance. Your symbolic design is now complete.

Let's learn about links

✿ **The Colour Wheel**: Ask the children a series of colour related questions: What kind of colour harmony is used here? Where else might you see red and yellow together? Take away the red ribbon. What colour harmony is used now? Are hues, tints, tones or shades used? How different would the arrangement look if you had used all tints or all shades instead of hues? What other yellow flowers can they think of that you could have used instead? When might you choose to use a monochromatic flower arrangement?

✿ **In the Pink or Got the Blues?**: Discuss how the colour yellow makes the children feel. What do they associate with yellow? What do they associate with the colour red? Take away the red ribbon. What difference has it made to the way the children respond to the arrangement?

✿ **Holocaust Symbolism**: Discuss the symbolism behind the arrangement. Flowers are used to represent many feelings and occasions, both happy and sad. They are also used in remembrance – for example, the red poppy is used to symbolise those who died in the First World War. In this contemporary arrangement, the colour yellow represents the many people who died in the Holocaust. The design is inspired by the story and symbolism in Ian McEwan's *Rose Blanche*: the forest that the main character walks through before stumbling across the concentration camp; the red ribbon she wears in the story; six yellow flowers to symbolise the six million Jews killed during this period; and the spiky-textured eryngium to reflect the harsh barbed wire.

Herbal Tussie-Mussie

This posy is scentsational! Learn how to spiral a bouquet using any combination of seasonal herbs and blooms, so long as it ends up wild and aromatic.

You can use one or two stems of lots of different flowers and foliage, or try adding grasses if you want a very dreamy effect. You can make the arrangement cheap or expensive, but make sure you include a few eye-catching flowers. Finish off by displaying the tussie-mussie in an easy-to-make container.

❀ First of all, lay out the flowers you want to use and cut the branching stems to make shorter stems. Once you have done this, remove two-thirds of the foliage from the stems, bottom up. This will give you a nice clean binding point – that is, the place where you tie your tussie-mussie. Clean stems will tie more easily, plus any leaves in or below the binding point will deteriorate in water, discolouring it and causing bacteria to form, which will shorten the life of your posy.

❀ To make a proper spiralled bouquet can be very tricky for adults, not to mention children. However, I have seen some great results from children who frequently do it much better and far more naturally than novice adults. I will explain how it is done, but if all else fails, just ask the children to make a soft fist and arrange the flowers inside their hand, expanding their fingers as the posy gets bigger.

❀ To spiral your tussie-mussie, the flowers go in your left hand, one at a time, if you are right-handed (and vice versa if you are left-handed). The job of the free hand is to add flowers or adjust the height of stems. Begin with your first flower and place it in your palm, with your thumb lightly holding it in place. This first flower is important as it dictates the height of your eventual posy: where your thumb crosses the stem is where you will end up tying the bouquet, so make sure you are happy with the position of the first stem. With your free hand, grab a stem of foliage and place this across the stem of the first flower in your hand at a slight angle and at an ever so slightly lower height than the original flower. Do the same again with another flower stem – that is, over the top of the last stem at a slight angle and at a slightly lower height. I usually find the 'flower plus foliage' pattern not only helps to keep the flower stems in place, but creates a balanced finished effect.

✿ When you've got four stems in your hand, grab the binding point with your free hand and slightly turn the posy clockwise in your left hand. Carry on spiralling your stems in the same way as before and turning your posy again after you have added another few stems. Keep doing this and you will quickly create a three-dimensional shape. The spiralled stems look neat and will allow you to move stems up or down easily if you need to adjust the height, as well as slotting in other flowers at the end if you feel there are gaps to be filled or misplaced flowers to be taken out and rearranged.

✿ When you are happy with your arrangement, wrap a length of raffia tightly around the binding point. Tie a firm knot or ask someone to do this for you. Trim off the excess raffia.

✿ Finally, trim the ends of the stems so that they are about half of the length of the arrangement above the binding point (thus making a third of the whole arrangement). You now have a wonderful herbal tussie-mussie!

Let's learn about links

✿ **The Colour Wheel**: Ask the children to identify the colour harmony in the tussie-mussie. What hues, tints, tones or shades are used?

✿ **In the Pink or Got the Blues?**: Discuss the psychological impact of the colours used in the tussie-mussie. Then get the children to consider which colours appear warmer or cooler and which colours appear nearer or further away.

✿ **Killers and Cures**: Herbal tussie-mussies were once believed to ward off disease. Encourage the children to find out what they can about the medicinal qualities of the herbs and sweet-smelling flowers.

✿ **A Career in Floristry**: Bouquets are incredibly popular in the floristry industry for weddings, Valentine's Day and Mother's Day. What flowers might the children use for each of these occasions? How and why might their choices differ? Ask them to find out what the latest trends are for wedding bouquets.

Making a container

This is a very cheap and effective way of making a container to pop your posy into if you wish!

Cut the stem and part of the rigid end of the aspidistra leaf. Place it smooth side down on your work surface and blob some glue here and there along the facing length of the leaf. Place your jam jar at the cut end of the leaf and roll. Secure the leaf further by wrapping raffia, wool or ribbon around the middle of the jar a couple of times, knot it and tie a bow. Fill with water and pop in your posy!

You will need:

Flowers and foliage

15–20 preserved stachys leaves

1 cymbidium orchid

1 stem of mimosa

1 stem of trailing amaranthus (this can be shared between two children)

1 stem of leucadendron

Equipment and sundries

1 plastic mask (you can buy these from art and craft shops)

Floristry scissors

Floristry glue

Mask Your Feelings

See how versatile flowers can be with this quick and easy tactile design. There is lots of glue involved, but stick with it and you will create a decadent mask to hide the real you.

✤ Begin by glueing the preserved stachys leaves on to the mask to create a base. Start from the outer edges, slightly overlapping the leaves each time until you almost meet in the middle. Tuck any excess from the leaves under the mask or through the eyes and trim the stems if you wish. Finish by glueing the leaves on to the middle section. In this way you will achieve a symmetrical and neat finish to your mask.

❀ Decorate half of the mask with your floral material. Start by glueing the mimosa leaves and leucadendron leaves on to the top corners. Next, create 'tassels' by glueing on the trailing amaranthus and mimosa flowers. As mimosa flowers are quite stiff, you could also place some in an upward direction, creating a nice line in your design for the eye to follow.

❀ Finally, glue on your focal cymbidium orchid. Make sure the stem is cut as short as possible and glue the petals, rather than the stem of the orchid. This will make it more secure on your mask. Wait for the glue to dry and wear it – you will look great!

Variation

Make it symmetrical and decorate both halves of the mask. Use the mimosa to decorate around the eye area.

Let's learn about links

✿ **The Colour Wheel**: Ask the children to name the colour harmony used in the mask and to identify the tints, tones, shades and hues.

✿ **In the Pink or Got the Blues?**: Ask the children what impact the colours have on the way they view the person behind the mask. What might the mask say about the wearer?

✿ **Let's Celebrate**: Masks are often used during celebrations, carnivals and festivals. Invite the children to make and wear their own mask during the class or school's own festival of flowers celebrations!

You will need:

Flowers and foliage

Couple of large handfuls of straw

Couple of handfuls of Spanish moss (or you could use sisal instead)

1 stem of waxflower

1 or 2 stems of spray chrysanthemum 'Skye'

1 stem of spray chrysanthemum 'Feeling Green'

Equipment and sundries

30 cm wire frame ring

Reel wire

Decorative wire

Floristry scissors

Floristry glue

Narrow ribbon

1 wooden dove (these are laser cut and can be purchased from craft shops)

Peace Wreath

Learn to bind with different types of wires and make an inexpensive wreath that lasts for ages and looks wonderful hanging on a wall.

❀ Decide where the top of your design is going to be and attach a loop of ribbon or wire to your wire frame. You will use this to hang your wreath on the wall.

❀ Next, bind the straw to the wire frame to make a good solid base on which to glue your flowers. Do this by placing a small handful of straw on top of the ring and binding it with your reel wire. You only need to put the straw on one side of the wire ring. Keep repeating this action, working around the frame until your wreath is covered with straw and all the wire is covered. The more straw you apply, the thicker your wreath will be. Cut the wire and tuck in the end. Give the straw a bit of a haircut until it all looks fairly neat.

✿ Repeat the previous step, but this time with the Spanish moss on top of the straw, and use decorative wire rather than reel wire. It's up to you how thickly you want the moss to be applied – my personal preference is to see a little bit of straw through the moss as it adds texture and creates a more rustic look, but experiment and see what you prefer.

✿ Now your base is ready, you can think about gluing the flowers on to your wreath. Cut the chrysanthemums as close to the base of the flower as you can and snip the waxflower into small stems – cut little stems of the foliage too as it looks good and will add texture to your design.

✿ Before gluing, play with pattern by placing the flowers on the wreath first. Put the larger flowers on top of the ring and the smaller flowers or buds on the inner and outer sides of your wreath. This will help the eye move around your design, with the focal point remaining in the centre line. Also, when you look at your wreath side on, you will be able to see flowers and foliage rather than just straw!

✿ When you are happy with your pattern, glue the flowers on by popping a little bit of floristry glue on to the back of the chrysanthemum flowers and the stalks of the waxflower. The waxflower will insert easily into the straw, but the glue gives it that little bit of extra security. You have now created your own peace wreath to give to a friend, family member or to keep for yourself.

✿ Don't forget to place your dove on the wreath too. Mine is hanging down, but you could glue it on instead.

Let's learn about links

❀ **The Colour Wheel**: Ask the children to identify what kind of colour harmony is used in the arrangement.

❀ **In the Pink or Got the Blues?**: What associations do the children make with the colours used in the wreath? Would this be the same for all cultures? What colours do they think symbolise war?

❀ **Peace in Our Time**: Discuss how the wreath has been designed to symbolise peace: the inclusion of the dove, the choice of colours – green and white, and the selection of flowers – chrysanthemums are said to symbolise the sun, and are therefore givers of life, while waxflowers represent lasting love or patience.

❀ **A Career in Floristry**: Wreaths are very popular at Christmas time. Ask the children to change the colour scheme and make their own door wreath in December.

Variation

When the flowers have passed their best, simply pick them off and add some fresh ones. For the background I have used Spanish moss, which adds a vintage, rustic look to the design. However, if you would like a more colourful and vibrant design, sisal works just as well.

You will need:

Flowers and foliage

3 stems of standard chrysanthemum 'Shamrock' (the lime-green colour is important in this arrangement as it acts as a unifier for all the other vibrant colours in the design)

3 stems of hot-pink standard carnation

3 stems of craspedia

3 stems of orange gerbera

3 stems of *Panicum virgatum* (fountain grass)

Equipment and sundries

2 strips of cardboard approximately 10 cm x 55 cm

4 180-gauge wires no more than 55 cm in length

Double-sided sticky tape

2 pieces of brightly coloured organza or fabric large enough to wrap around each cardboard strip

Stapler

Wool

Decorative wire

Selection of buttons

9 lengths of paper-covered wire

9 test tubes (plastic are cheaper than glass)

6 Midelino sticks

Test Tubes

Experiment with bright colours in this souped-up, sci-fi, pop art arrangement, proving there is more than one way to keep flowers alive (inspired by a Jessica and Victoria Richards design).

❀ To make your frame, lay out both strips of cardboard and place two of the 180-gauge wires on top of each piece so they look like train lines. Cover the gauge wires with double-sided sticky tape. Remove the backing and wrap your chosen piece of material around each strip of cardboard. Don't worry about any flaps of material – you will bind these in with the decorative wire and wool later on.

❀ Staple your two pieces of cardboard together at the ends only, with the best sides facing outwards.

✿ Wrap wool and/or decorative wire around the cardboard to decorate and bind the two pieces together. Go backwards and forwards a couple of times and lengthways too if you wish. Knot the wool when you have finished and glue a few buttons down both sides of the short edges of the cardboard to hide your staples.

✿ Bend the cardboard into your desired shape, which should be stable when standing up, and briefly put to one side as you prepare your test tubes.

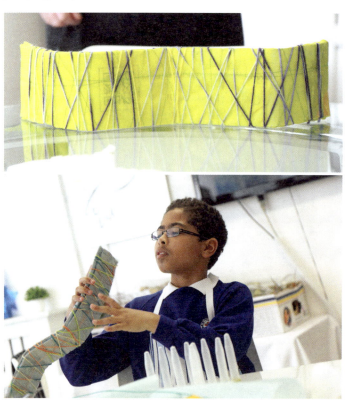

✿ Decorate the test tubes with wool. Leaving a little extra length to knot at the end, wrap the wool around and down the tube and then back up again. Knot the ends and cut off any excess. Do this for each test tube. You could use one colour wool or a mix of colours if you like.

❀ Next, make the wire test tube holders. Take a length of paper covered wire and, placing the top of a test tube in the middle of the wire, twist the wire once or twice and bend the rest down the length of the test tube to create a spine. Cut off any wire that hangs below the test tube. Push the wire spine into the top of your frame in the gap between the two pieces of cardboard. Place the test tubes in groups and at slightly varying heights to add interest to your design.

❀ Fill the test tubes with water and insert your flowers and grass. You can put more than one flower in a test tube.

❀ For a final bit of flair, insert your Midelino sticks into the test tubes to create another point of interest.

Let's learn about links

❀ **The Colour Wheel**: Ask the children to discuss what kind of colour harmony is used here. Would they change any of the colours?

❀ **In the Pink or Got the Blues?**: How would the children describe the temperature of these colours? Do the colours remind them of anything they have seen before?

❀ **Flowers in Art**: What style of art do these colours remind the children of? Get them to look at some pop art paintings and decide which one this arrangement would most comfortably sit next to in an art gallery.

❀ **Staying Alive**: Ask the children what principles of science are applied in this design to help the flowers stay alive. What else could they do as florists to help this arrangement live as long as possible? Why will these cut flowers eventually die?

Woodland Wall Hanging

Use nature as your inspiration and create a wonderfully textured piece of floral art using seeds, cones, bark, moss – anything you can get your hands on.

❀ Begin by making the outside frame. I have gone for a 30 cm wide by 40 cm long frame here, but you can make this any size you like. So, using your secateurs, cut two strong twigs of 30 cm in length and two of 40 cm.

❀ Bind the corners together with reel wire. When binding the corners, place the two longer pieces on top of the shorter pieces as you will find it hangs better on the wall if the shorter piece (to which you will attach the hanging loop) is closer to the wall. Also, leave a little of the twig lengths projecting at the sides. This gives a rustic feel to the piece and makes binding the corners easier. Don't worry if your frame wiggles a little at this point.

❀ Next, decide whether you will fix the twigs on top of the outside frame or behind it. It is best to choose one or the other, and stick to it, as it lends a more professional finish. However, it is no matter if twigs end up wired in front as well as behind the outside frame – it will still look lovely.

❖ Start wiring the internal twigs to the frame. Begin with two strong twigs, to act as your struts, placed diagonally within the frame. Continue in this manner with all the other varieties of twigs and twine you have collected. Where twigs cross within the frame, wire these together as well – it will make your frame stronger and neater. Once your frame is complete and feels robust and rigid, cut off any straggly ends with floristry scissors or secateurs.

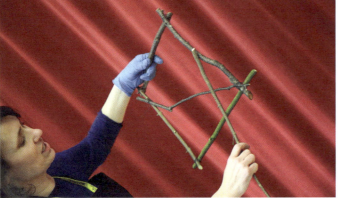

❖ Aiming for a fluid diagonal line, glue the three pieces of bark on to the internal twigs. Try to find a place where you will have enough twig to make sure the bark will remain secure. If in doubt, you can always use reel wire to attach it to the twigs. You will not see any of the wire later as it will be covered with flowers.

❀ You are now ready to add foliage, cones, berries, moss and flowers. Begin with the foliage and, thinking in groups and lines, work in two relaxed diagonals, grouping the foliage along these lines. Glue one leaf type along one diagonal line and another leaf type along the other. Small pieces of fern can be glued along both diagonals to link the two lines together.

❀ Now group and glue on the focal pieces – in this case, the rose hips along one diagonal and the chrysanthemums along the other. When cutting the flowers, make sure you cut as near to the base as you can as it will adhere better if there is little or no stem attached. Do the same for the filler pieces – the horse chestnut cases, the ivy berries and haws.

✿ Wire in a few small pine cones, glue the odd little piece of moss here and there to complete the scene, and you have your very own unique woodland wall hanging!

✿ Finally, to hang on the wall, make a loop from either reel wire, thick string or decorative ribbon.

Let's learn about links

✿ **The Colour Wheel:** Discuss with the children what kind of colour harmony is used here.

✿ **In the Pink or Got the Blues?:** Ask the children what the colours in this arrangement remind them of. Do they like the colours?

✿ **Change and Transition:** Use the woodland wall hanging to examine change and transition in the life of a plant: from seed to flower to fruit.

✿ **Flowers in Art:** Many artists use nature and natural materials – for example, Andy Goldsworthy, Chris Drury and Tada Asuka. Encourage the children to find out what they can about these artists and their work. They could research land and environmental art or look at artists who work with collage and assemblage. They could then decide in which area of art the woodland wall hanging belongs.

✿ **The Birds and the Bees:** As a range of seeds, berries and flowers are used in this arrangement, it would be an ideal platform from which to discuss the different stages in a plant's life, including seed dispersal.

✿ **Where the Wild Things Are:** Ask the children to look at all the natural materials used in the woodland wall hanging. What are the characteristics of this habitat? Where in the world would they expect to find this habitat? What else might they find in a wood? Why are woodlands important?

You will need:

Flowers and foliage

3 stems of *Cyperus alternifolius*

3 stems of leucadendron 'Safari Sunset'

2 stems of *Brunia albiflora*

5 stems of spray chrysanthemum 'Feeling Green'

10 stems of dianthus 'Green Trick'

3 stems of pink *Anigozanthos fuliginosus*

1 stem of *Asparagus umbellatus* (ming fern), or you could use 1 stem of *Rumohra adiantiformis* (leather leaf)

Equipment and sundries

18 cm foam posy pad

Strip of felt 4 cm x 60 cm

3 foam hemispheres (buy the small 7 cm spheres and cut them in half)

Kebab sticks or German pins

Floristry glue

Floristry scissors

Sisal

Decorative wire

Yellow split peas

Wild rice

Fantasy Island

Create your own fantasy habitat fit for a wild thing, and learn the skill of basing at the same time!

✿ Place the posy pad foam side down into water and let it soak for a while. Remove and shake off excess water. Cover the lower part of the pad with felt.

✿ Begin to make the tree canopy of your design. Insert your three tall cyperus in a scalene triangle, staggering the heights slightly to create interest.

✿ Now create three hillocks by placing your spheres on the posy pad, again forming a triangle, and secure in place by driving a kebab stick through the centre of the sphere and well into the posy pad. Cut off any excess. Alternatively, secure the base with German pins, making sure you insert into both the dome and the pad.

✿ Begin to base your three domes with the chrysanthemum and dianthus. To do this, cut the flowers (leaving about 2 cm of stem) and, beginning at the top of your dome, push in the stem as far as it will go so that the flower is lying flat against the foam. Insert another flower next to it, avoiding leaving a gap between the two. Keep going until the dome is covered. Basing around the sides of the posy pad too will give a wild, unrestrained look to your island.

✿ Next, insert the anigozanthos and the brunia into the posy pad in the same way as above. You can make more brunia stems by splitting them in half. Then insert the leucadendron and finish off by filling any gaps with the asparagus.

❀ You are now ready to make your wild thing! Take a handful of sisal and tease it into the size and shape of your creature. Use the decorative wire to create horns, head, neck, arms, body and legs —or however you imagine your wild thing to look. Glue on split peas for eyes and wild rice for teeth and claws. Finally, place your wild thing in your arrangement … is it hiding in the bushes or having fun hanging from a tree?

Let's learn about links

✿ **The Colour Wheel:** How would the children describe the colour scheme used in your arrangement? What tints, tones, shades or hues are used?

✿ **In the Pink or Got the Blues?:** How do the colours in this arrangement make the children feel about the island?

✿ **Where the Wild Things Are:** Ask the children the following questions: Where in the world do the flowers and foliage you have used come from? In what kinds of conditions do they like to grow? How would they describe the habitat you have created? How far does it resemble the setting in Maurice Sendak's story, *Where the Wild Things Are*? What else do they imagine they might find in your fantasy island habitat?

Fabulous Flower Badge

Wow with a vanda orchid as you learn to make a popular commercial floral arrangement! I've seen boys who have set out to give their badge to their mum deciding instead to keep it for themselves!

❀ Begin by making the base. Lay the aspidistra leaf on the table, smooth side down, so the spine of the leaf is facing up. Glue one side of the cardboard square and place this near the tip of the leaf, glue side down. Take the tip of the leaf, fold it over the cardboard square, and then keep folding the square over until the leaf is wrapped at least once around the cardboard. If the leaf isn't too stiff, you can wrap it around again before you cut off the tough section of the leaf and stem. Glue the underside of the last bit of aspidistra down.

❧ Decide how you want your badge to look – square or diamond – then glue the flat side of your corsage badge to the least attractive side of your leaf. Now you are ready to decorate your badge.

❧ Snip the China grass at a 45 degree angle, or loop it, and glue it to the top of your flower badge. Try to position it to one side, rather than in the middle, as this will make a more interesting and fluid design.

❧ Next, glue the sisal to the badge, spreading it widely over the base. You can even cascade your sisal down into a point, which is what I sometimes like to do. Whichever way you choose, make sure you can see some of the sisal behind your flower and that the end result looks delicate rather than clumpy. A little sisal goes an extraordinarily long way.

✿ Glue the vanda orchid to your flower badge, placing it centrally with the tongue looking at you and facing south. To help the flower stick better to your badge, glue the base of the petals rather than where the stem was.

✿ Next, stick the ornithogalum flowers on to your badge. If you are cascading your sisal, the flowers look very pretty glued cascading down too and stick amazingly well to little bits of sisal. If you decide to do this, as I have, then make

sure your flower size decreases the further down the sisal you go. To help the design and movement of the eye, think big in the middle and small at the edges.

✿ Once your badge is completely dry, wear it with pride!

Variation

You could adapt this design and create a bracelet instead. Use a Velcro wristlet instead of the badge and substitute feathers for the aspidistra and cardboard.

Let's learn about links

❀ **The Colour Wheel:** Discuss the colour harmony used in the arrangement. What do the children like about the colours used?

❀ **In the Pink or Got the Blues?:** Ask the children what the colours suggest about the wearer. How would a different colour flower or sisal impact on the look of the badge?

❀ **A Career in Floristry:** Badges, corsages and bracelets are very popular for weddings. Ask the children to discuss what type of wedding the badge might be suitable for. How could they adapt it to suit a range of different people?

Chapter 8
Let's learn about ...

The Colour Wheel

Aprons at the ready as the children explore the world of colour and colour schemes!

Main subjects covered

Art and design
Maths (if you get the children making their own colour wheel)
English

Resources you might need

Jars of water
Red, yellow, blue, white and black paints
Mixing palette
Slim-tipped paintbrushes
Colour wheel templates (or compasses, protractors and rulers)
Painting paper

Some useful words you might like to use

Analogous
Colour harmony
Complementary colours
Connotation
Contrast
Hue
Monochromatic
Near complementary
Polychromatic
Primary colours
Secondary colours
Segments
Shade

Split complementary
Tertiary colours
Tetradic
Tint
Tone
Triadic
Value

And if using a compass and protractor

Angles
Diameter
Radius

The session

1   Show the children an example of a colour wheel and inform them that it was invented by a great scientist, Sir Isaac Newton, and is used to visually display the relationships between primary, secondary and tertiary colours and their corresponding tints, tones and shades.

2   Tell the children that they are now going to create a colour wheel of their own, exploring how different colours are made. Hand out templates to the children if you have them, or they could create their own using a compass, protractor and ruler. They could even try making a flower-shaped colour wheel, each segment being a petal.

> **Variation:** How far you go with this exercise will depend on the age and ability of the children. For example, you could have a wheel that examines just primary and secondary colours or hues, rather than delving into tints, tones and shades. I would encourage you to challenge your students though!

3   First of all, show the children the colours red, yellow and blue, preferably using real flowers or pictures of flowers. Explain that these three colours are called primary colours – primary meaning 'first' or 'most important'. These three colours are 'true' colours and cannot be created by mixing other colours.

4   Ask the children to paint in the primary colours in the correct position on the colour wheel (i.e. on the very outside edge, making sure they leave three empty segments between each colour). Remind the children not to rush and to be as neat and careful as they can when painting in the colours. It is important that they try to keep within the lines of each segment.

> **Note:** Encourage the children to use a slim-tipped brush as this task involves quite delicate painting. Remind them to clean their brush in water before dipping into the next paint colour – we want to keep the colours as pure as possible. It also helps to have a cloth handy which the children can use to dry their paintbrush on before they start on the next paint colour. This ensures that the colours remain vibrant and the paint isn't too watery or diluted (chroma is the name for the strength of colour). It also avoids running between colours. It is worthwhile demonstrating good practice and perhaps showing the poor results of bad practice!

5   Next, ask the children to begin mixing the primary colours and see what happens. Yellow and blue produce green, orange comes from yellow and red, and violet is made when red and blue are mixed together. Explain that these three new colours are called secondary colours. Ask the children where on the wheel they need to paint in the secondary colours. Green should be on the outside portion of the middle

segment between yellow and blue to show that it is the secondary made from these two primary colours. The children should be starting to see an illustrated relationship between the colours. Therefore, orange goes in-between yellow and red and violet goes in-between red and blue. Now let the children go ahead and paint in green, orange and violet.

> Note: Remind the children again to clean their paintbrush each time they want to use a different colour. Tell them that it is important to try and mix together equal quantities of paint for a truer secondary colour.

6   Now get the children making the six tertiary colours, achieved by mixing a primary and a secondary together. Thankfully, the mixes are evident in the names of the tertiary colours: red-orange, yellow-orange, yellow-green, blue-green, blue-violet and red-violet. Again, ask the children where the logical position of the tertiary colours would be on the colour wheel: yellow-orange goes in the outer edge of the segment between yellow and orange! Easy! Start painting!

> Note: Tertiary colour names always begin with the primary colour name first followed by the secondary colour. They know their places! Keep reminding the children about the importance of a clean brush. Again, they should try to mix equal quantities of primary and secondary colours to get a truer tertiary colour.

7   Explain to the children that what they have just created on the outside edge of each segment of the colour wheel are the hues – colours created by mixing with other colours. Now they are going to create tints, tones and shades. This is the alteration of the hues value (lightness and darkness) by adding white, grey and black respectively.

8   Give the children white and black paints and ask them to first of all create tints, then tones, then shades for each of the hues and paint them in the appropriate places on the colour wheel. Generally, tints are placed under the hues, tones under tints and then finally shades.

> Note: To create grey, mix equal quantities of white and black paint. The children should do this in a large quantity so that there is enough to use with all twelve colours. This will make the tones more consistent. Don't worry too much if they run out though, just get them to make some more!

> Extension: The children could create their own colour chart, like the ones you find in DIY stores, and experiment with the value of one particular colour, say the tints of blue. Keep adding more and more white and see how the value of the colour changes.

9   Explain that how we combine the twelve different hues and their tints, tones and shades is called colour harmony. Understanding colour harmony is important when creating arrangements for a particular place, person, mood or purpose.

10 Tell the children they are now going to investigate the nine different colour harmonies. The children will work in groups of three and will be handed three different sets of cards (see pages 112–116). The first set of cards will have the nine different colour harmonies named on each one. A second set will have the definition of the colour harmonies. A third set will have examples from the colour wheel highlighting a particular colour harmony. Ask the children to match colour harmonies with their definitions and examples.

11 As a next step, the children could find pictures of flower arrangements from the internet, magazines or books that illustrate each colour harmony. These could be cut out or copied and placed next to their cards.

12 Once they have done this, ask the children to describe their emotional responses to each colour harmony, with one person in each group to be a scribe. Next, they should compare and consider the advantages and disadvantages of each colour harmony – what kind of place, event, person or mood might they be suitable for?

> **Variation:** Instead, or as well as the colour wheel set of cards, the children could identify an example of each colour harmony from their own colour wheel.

13 Using a selection of flowers, ask the children to make different colour harmony bouquets and state who they would give them to and for what occasion.

14 Finally, end the session by discussing the children's favourite colour harmonies and why they like them. Ask them to create a floral arrangement showing a particular colour harmony which they could evaluate afterwards.

Some things you might like to discuss

✿ How important is colour in our lives?

✿ What is your favourite colour and why?

✿ How is colour used in our lives?

Learning to go: Invite the children to paint a picture. Using a colour harmony of their choice, ask them to paint a still life of a vase of real flowers. Then ask them to paint it again using a different colour harmony. Get the children to talk about their choices and describe the differences in mood of the two pieces as a result of the different colour harmonies used. Use the following questions to prompt discussion: Were you trying to capture a particular mood? If so, did your choices work? When they are painting, get them to look really closely at their subject and show the tints, tones and shades.

Variation: You could also give the children a remit for their painting – for example, a word such as tranquil or wild.

Extra English: Paint a flower poem! Read the children a poem or a selection of poems about flowers and ask them to consider what colour certain words and phrases would be. Ask them what colour harmony they would use to 'paint the poem' – then let them paint it!

A fraction of maths: Using their flower colour wheel, ask the children to work on angles, arcs, segments, radii, pi, diameter and circumference.

The colour harmony cards

Colour harmony	Definition	Colour wheel
Monochromatic	Mono, meaning one, is the use of hues, tints, tones and shades from one segment of the colour wheel only	
Analogous	This harmony is made up of three or four colours next to one another on the colour wheel which share a primary colour. You cannot have more than one primary colour in an analogous scheme	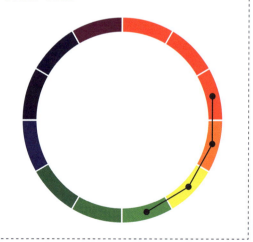

Colour harmony	Definition	Colour wheel
Complementary	Two colours that sit directly opposite one another on the colour wheel	
Colour harmony	Definition	Colour wheel
Split complementary	A three colour combination. This harmony is made up of one colour on the colour wheel and the two colours on either side of its complementary colour. There will always be at least one tertiary in this combination	

Colour harmony	**Definition**	**Colour wheel**
Near complementary	A two colour combination. This harmony is achieved by taking a colour and one of the two colours either side of its complementary	
Colour harmony	**Definition**	**Colour wheel**
Triadic	Three colours equidistant apart on the colour wheel	

Colour harmony	Definition	Colour wheel
Tetradic	Four colours equidistant apart on the colour wheel	
Contrast	A two colour harmony. This harmony is obtained by counting! Pick one colour from the colour wheel and name it 1. Go either way on the wheel and count the next colour to it as 2, then the next along as 3 and the next as 4. When you reach 5, you have found your colour harmony colour!	

Colour harmony

Polychromatic

Definition

Using four or more colours and not following any previous colour harmony

Colour wheel

In the Pink or Got the Blues?

The children will learn all about the properties and influences of colour and consider its emotional, psychological and symbolic impact on us. This session assumes you have covered 'The Colour Wheel' first.

Main subjects covered

Art and design

Maths

English

Resources

Colour wheel

Examples of still-life flower paintings by the Dutch masters

Sugar paper

Paints

Brushes

Water jars

Palettes

Some useful words you might like to use

Connotation

Luminosity

Representation

Symbolism

Temperature

Value

The session

1   Remind the children of the colour wheel and explain that the first property they are going to investigate is temperature. Give the children a selection of hues, either on cards or as flowers, and ask them to place the cards or flowers into two piles: colours they think are warm and colours they consider to be cool. Discuss the results and show them the temperature colour wheel below.

Warm Colours | Cool Colours

> Note: You may find differences in the temperature of the colour wheels you find on the internet: some include red-violet or yellow-green as warm, some as cold. You could discuss this with the class and ask them what they think is the best fit for these two colours.

2   Discuss why colour temperature is important and where or when it might be used. Temperature is crucial to design work as it creates a sense of depth: the warm colours seem to come forward or advance, while the cool colours recede. Colours at the warmer end of the spectrum are psychologically more dynamic, bright, energetic, fiery and passionate, and draw attention to themselves in a way that cooler colours do not. As a result, they can become tiring to the eye, so caution must be taken when considering where and how they are used. Cool colours are calm, serene and easy on the eye and are more suitable for smaller areas as they create a sense of space and do not dominate.

3   Ask the children to collect pictures of flowers showing examples of warm and cool colours and then get them to write the best, most accurate descriptive words they can find next to each picture. The pictures the children collect could be arranged on the classroom wall or stuck, scrapbook style, into their art or exercise books.

> Variation: Play a game with colour temperature, holding up two different coloured flowers and asking the children to decide which flower appears nearer or further away.

4   Painting time! Decide on two colours – one warm and one cool – and experiment a little. On two separate pieces of paper, ask the children to draw a picture of a flower or a leaf, making it as big or as small as they like but roughly identical

in size on each piece of paper. On the first piece of paper the flower should be painted in the warm colour and the background in the cool colour. On the second piece of paper the flower is painted in the cool colour and the background in the warm colour. What difference has the change of colours made to the depiction of the flower? What difference has it made to the way the children react to the flower? Which do they prefer and why? Display the children's artwork on the wall.

> Extension: You could ask the children to refer back to colour harmonies here and ask them what colour harmonies are being displayed when a cool and warm colour are put together.

5 The next property the children are going to learn about is luminosity, the term used to describe the amount of light emitted from a colour. With the children working in small groups, hand out some examples of famous Dutch master flower paintings and ask the groups to identify the most luminous parts of each of the paintings. Then ask them to identify the least luminous. From a colour point of view, what do they notice about the most luminous/least luminous parts of the paintings? How did the artist achieve such effects?

> Note: It might be helpful for the children to have their colour wheel at hand during this activity.

6 If it hasn't already arisen in observation, experiment or discussion, explain that tints are the most luminous as they contain white and work better in dim light than pure hues, shades (which contain black) and tones (which contain grey). The lighter colours are referred to as advancing colours, with the most luminous properties found in yellow, followed by orange, yellow-green, pale pink and peach. The darker colours of blue, violet, green, red and purple have low luminosity and will appear to recede. These should be avoided in large areas and, from a floral point of view, in big church flower displays.

> Extension: How can understanding the luminous powers of colour help the painter, the florist, the photographer, the interior designer, make-up artist or jewellery designer?

7 Now explore the influence of colour. Working in eight different groups, give each group one colour to respond to from red, yellow, blue, green, violet, orange, black and white. First of all, nominate a scribe and ask them to write down any words or word associations that the children can think of about that colour on a piece of sugar paper. For example, white might elicit answers like wedding dress or

funeral clothing (depending on culture), innocence, snow or cold. Other areas to consider could be emotional effect, psychological impact, significant dates or events of the year, anniversaries, cultural influences, countries and symbols.

8   Give each group a few minutes to do this before they carousel to the next colour, read what has been previously written and add further words if appropriate. They should do this for all eight colours, then discuss the results as a class. Did anything that had been written surprise anyone? How far do they agree/disagree with some of the words? Using the internet or the library, what more can they find out about the emotional and psychological impact of colours? They could collect pictures to evidence their ideas, including pictures of flowers, of course.

9   Finally, the children could create their own floral arrangement and give it a 'mood' title. They should ask a friend to evaluate its temperature, luminosity and the emotional and psychological effect its colour has on them – would they give it a different 'mood' title?

Some things you might like to discuss

❀   How important is colour in our lives?

❀   What is your favourite colour and why?

❀   How is colour used in our lives?

❀   Where do colour associations come from?

❀   Why might colour symbolism differ from culture to culture?

❀   How do some colours come to symbolise certain things – for example, why is the Jewish Star of David yellow?

Learning to go: Ask the children to create a colour mood board with pictures of flowers or flower arrangements cut out from magazines or printed from the internet. Their mood board could even be created in the shape of a flower!

Extra English: Get the children to think about how colour appears in the phrases we use – for example, 'seeing red' or 'got the blues'. Ask them to note down their ideas and write a 'colour poem' or short descriptive paragraph including as many phrases as possible.

A fraction of maths: Place a selection of different coloured flowers in box or covered bucket and work out the probability of pulling out a particular colour. Then consider the probability of whether the next flower to be pulled out will be more or less luminous or of a cool or warm temperature. The more variety of colours you have, the trickier it is to work out the probability.

Change and Transition

Change and transition happens to all of us in our lives, but when important shifts occur do we know how to make a successful transition? Children will learn about the essential differences between the two words, understand the many stages of transition and learn how to manage them.

This 'Let's learn about ...' is very useful to do with children when they are about to move to a new school – for example, primary to secondary or elementary to high school – and will be a memorable feature of any transition work that you and partner schools may do.

Main subjects covered

PSHE   Maths
Science   English

Resources you might need

Future and present questions
Images showing the development of a plant
(from seed to seedling)
Images showing the development of a flower
(from bud to bloom)
Sugar paper
Felt pens

Some useful words you might like to use

Acceptance   Flower
Anxiety   Hostility
Bloom   Petals
Blossom   Psychological
Change   Psychology
Complacency   Seed
Denial   Seedling
Disillusionment   Transition

The session

1   Consider changes in life – perhaps ask the children to write down what changes can occur in people's lives. Some examples might be a change of hairstyle, clothes, jobs, schools, friends and house. Explain to the children that change is situational – it can happen quickly and it can happen with or without transition. Tell them to put this aside for now, but assure them that you will come back to it later.

2   Show the children images of the different stages of a plant's growth from seed to seedling. Label each stage of seed development with a phase that corresponds with the children's journey through school so far. For example, a seedling just emerging could be home and nursery, a slighter bigger seedling with a few roots could be the first two years at school, a seedling with its first leaves and more roots could be the next two years at school and so on, ending with a question mark to signify the next step. As you reveal each stage of development, add narration explaining how the seed's growth reflects their own development in school until this point.

3   Ask the children what they think will happen to the seedling next. How might the seed's next step relate to their own life? What are their expectations of their own development? What are the expectations of others about their own development?

4   At this point, split the class into small groups of say three or four. To half of the groups, hand out a set of questions about the present for them to consider. For example:

   ❀   What have you enjoyed about being at primary school?

   ❀   What do you think you will miss when you move to secondary school?

   ❀   How has primary school helped to get you ready for your life ahead?

   ❀   What do you think you will gain from the change?

   ❀   Are you nervous about the change?

To the other half, give out a set of questions about the future. For example:

   ❀   What are your hopes about secondary school?

   ❀   What are your aspirations for the future beyond secondary school?

   ❀   What can you do to make your hopes a reality?

   ❀   What can others do to help you?

5   Give the children time to consider and discuss the questions, and then ask them to note down all their ideas on a large piece of sugar paper.

6 Next, ask the groups to swap questions and notes so that those who initially worked on the future are now working on the present, and vice versa. Can the children add anything further to the notes? Discuss these ideas as a whole class.

7 Show the children pictures of the developing stages of a flower from bud to bloom – for example, a sunflower. Ask the children to imagine they are this sunflower. By the end of secondary or high school, the children should be in a position where they are blooming or about to bloom. But how will this happen? Hand out copies of the developing stages of the blooming flower to each child and ask them, individually, to assess their present skills against the flower. For example, where are they currently in maths or English? Are they still a tightly closed bud or are their petals beginning to emerge? And how about music? Dance? Listening? Working with others? Managing deadlines? Eating healthily?

8 Give the children another copy of the blooming flower picture, but this time ask them to annotate where they would like to be with these skills in the future. How many of the skills would they need to develop to feel that they could be in a position to eventually bloom as an individual?

Variation: 'The future' could mean many futures – one year, the end of secondary or high school, as an adult and so on.

9 Show a picture of a dying flower and explain that this is what the children should avoid when they change environments. Discuss how they can avoid the 'dying flower'

syndrome. How did the plant become so sorry? What does a plant need to blossom and bloom? What will they need to blossom and bloom? What do they need to do to avoid ending up like a shrivelled, dying flower?

10 Explain that transition is psychological and can involve a range of feelings. What is important is how we react to change, which is often a gradual process, although some people may make a quicker transition than others. Successful transition is dependent on our nature – how willing we are to help ourselves, what efforts we are prepared to put in and how we can exploit the resources around us. Return to the first activity on change and ask the children to rank the changes according to what will involve the greater or lesser transition.

Variation: You might like to show the children a Fisher's personal transition curve, highlighting the range of feelings they may expect to experience and considering what they could do at each point to help themselves.

11 Finally, transition in size, space or colour is key to an interesting arrangement in floristry. Ask the children to show one aspect of this in a floral arrangement and evaluate how it could symbolise their own transition in life.

Some things you might like to discuss

✿ Talk about a time when you experienced change. How were you effected?

✿ Do you recognise anything about yourself from the Fisher's personal transition curve?

✿ What changes have you found easy in life?

✿ What changes did you find difficult?

✿ Discuss with a friend, or reflect on your own, the consequences – good and bad – of any of your actions or behaviours when change occurred. What have you learned from them?

Learning to go: Change and transition happens to all living things. Ask the children to choose a flower and find out about the different stages of its life cycle and the transition from seed to flower. Consider what happens to the stems, the leaves, the buds and the flowers as it grows. How do they change in shape, thickness and number? How tall do they usually grow? How many flowers does the plant produce? What do the buds look like compared to the flower? What influences the rate at which a flower develops? Which plant takes the longest to develop a flower? How does the change and transition of a flower compare to that of a human?

Extra English: Get the children to make their own personal 'Change and Transition' scrapbook. They could draw in a timeline and stick in photos of themselves so far (e.g. as a baby or toddler), with some silhouettes going forward to be filled in later. The scrapbook could also include stories and reflections on changes that have occurred, happiest memories or significant moments in their life, and finish with what hopes they have for the future.

A fraction of maths: Invite the children to plant a seed and make a hypothesis about its rate of growth and what date they predict it will flower. Track its progress, measuring and recording its growth stages on a calendar. Use the following questions: How tall is it at different times? Work out how much it has grown. Round numbers up or down to the nearest centimetre. How does your plant's progress compare to that of a friend's? If your friend's plant is making greater progress, consider what changes you could make to how you care for your plant to make it grow quicker and healthier. Finally, was your hypothesis correct?

Flowers in Art

Children don't have to cut off an ear to enjoy flowers in art, but they will look at an artist who did and some of his very famous paintings. They will also look at artists who decided to keep both their ears!

Main subjects covered

English	ICT
Art and design	Maths

Resources

ICT
Examples of flower paintings
Pencils
Paper
Paints

Some useful words you might like to use

Atmosphere
Composition
Depiction
Elements (e.g. colour, line, shape, form, texture)
Mood
Scene

The session[1]

1   Explain to the children that they will be curators of their own virtual floral art exhibition – picking interesting and quality exhibits, researching and presenting biographical and contextual information about the artist and their work, and ending with the inclusion of a photo of their own art-inspired floral arrangement.

> **Variation and bold extension:** You could be really ambitious and make this a real exhibition to be held in the school hall, inviting parents and the local community to view the top ten paintings chosen by the children. The exhibition could include the children's own work relating to the paintings. This might include displays of rapid sketches, close studies, sequences of sketches using a diversity of drawing implements, shade and tone pictures, pictures of the flower paintings using a limited colour palette, experimentation with the quality of marks and finally, the pièce de résistance, flower arrangements inspired by the paintings. The children could keep a flower sketchbook to note down, sketch and reflect as they go along – this too could be part of the floral art exhibition.

2   With an eye on pace, show and discuss some of *The Observer*'s choices, eliciting initial responses from the children based on what they like or don't like about the painting.

You could use some of the following prompts to help guide discussion and to develop the way they look at a picture:

Initial response:

❀   What do you like/dislike about this painting?

❀   What do you see in this painting?

❀   What words would you use to describe this painting? What other words might you use?

❀   What did you notice first about this painting? What do you think the artist did to make you notice it? What else do you notice?

❀   How would you describe the lines in this picture? The shapes? The colours?

❀   How does this painting make you feel?

❀   How would you describe this painting to a person who could not see it?

❀   What might you see, hear, smell or feel if you were in the world of this painting?

❀   What words would you use to describe the mood of this painting?

Compare:

❀   Does this painting remind you of anything? If so, what?

---

1   This session was inspired by Laura Cumming, 'The 10 Best Flower Paintings – In Pictures', *The Observer* (8 April 2012). Available at: <http://www.theguardian.com/culture/gallery/2012/apr/08/the-10-best-flower-paintings>.

❀ What things do you recognise in this picture? What things seem new to you?

❀ How is this painting similar to or different from the one you just saw?

❀ How is this picture similar to or different from real life?

❀ Which painting do you find most interesting and why?

❀ Which is your favourite of the ten paintings and why?

❀ Have you seen anything like this before?

> **Variation:** Ask the children to work in groups. Call out one person from each group to look at a picture of a painting for ten seconds only. Instruct the person to go back and describe it to their group as well as they can. The groups' job is to try and quickly recreate it on a piece of sugar paper or any other drawing medium of your choice. After one minute, call out a different person to view the picture, but only give them six seconds to look. When they return to their group, they now have only thirty seconds to add to the picture. You can keep doing this, reducing the time as drastically, or not, as you feel fits the pace. At the end, ask the groups to display their results and, finally, show the painting to the whole class.

3 The final choice in *The Observer*'s top ten is van Gogh's *Vase with Pink Roses*, which they acknowledge is not as famous as his *Sunflowers* paintings. Show the children the rose and sunflowers pictures side by side and discuss and compare them, using some of the questions below to guide and shape their talk. Explain that they are going to look at the two paintings in more depth, learning how to view with a critical as well as an emotional eye.

Be critical:

❀ What objects appear close and which appear further away? What effect does this have?

❀ Describe the colours in this painting. What colour is used most? Why might that be? What do the colours suggest?

❀ Does this painting look crowded or spacious? Is it busy or plain? What effect does that have on the flower depicted in the painting?

❀ What do you think is the most important part of this painting? Why?

❀ What type of person do you think owns these flowers? Why?

❀ What do you notice about line, texture, form, composition and pattern? How do these aspects make you feel about the painting? Why do you think the artist chose to paint the flowers in this way?

❀ What changes would you make to the painting? How might it affect the way you view the picture?

❀ What questions would you ask the artist about this work, if he were here?

❀ Why do you suppose the artist made this painting?

❀ What do you think might be the message or theme?

❀ What do you think is the viewpoint of the artist?

Explain:

❀ Rename the painting and describe the reasons for your choice.

❀ What do you think is happening in this painting? What else could be happening?

❀ What world is this painting a part of? What is going on beyond the borders of this painting?

❀ Who might the flowers belong to?

❀ What do you think this painting is about? How did you arrive at that idea?

❀ What might it be like to live in this painting?

❀ How do you think the artist feels about the flowers he has painted? What makes you believe that?

Evaluate:

❀ What do you think is good/bad about this painting?

❀ Why do you think other people should/should not see this work of art?

❀ What do you think is worth remembering about this painting?

❀ Why do you think this painting is so valued?

❀ This particular painting was not highly regarded when van Gogh was alive. Why do you think that is? What might have changed people's minds?

❀ Why do you think *Sunflowers* is the more famous painting? Is it a 'better' painting? Does it deserve to be more famous? Which one do you prefer?

4 Now show the children a bunch of beautiful sunflowers and ask them to compare the real-life sunflowers with van Gogh's painted sunflowers. Use some of the prompt questions to encourage the children to respond to the flowers, and then ask what they think van Gogh saw as he looked at them. What qualities of the sunflower has he captured in his painting? How has he done this? What are the similarities and differences between the real and the painted sunflower?

5 Ask the children to research the life of van Gogh and look at some of his other flower paintings. How does this new knowledge affect the way they view *Vase with Pink Flowers* and *Sunflowers*? What influenced his style? How would they describe his style? How has he achieved his style? Do they like his paintings?

6 Now that the children have some idea and experience of responding to and evaluating paintings, tell them that it is now over to them to begin the job of curating. Using Pinterest or a scrapbook style, ask them to look through books and the internet for examples of paintings of flowers and to collect those that they find interesting or that they like, and be prepared to discuss their choices. You could give the children

a selection of names from the following list of artists to look up (some are famous for flower paintings while others included flowers within their oeuvre): Georgia O'Keefe, Joan Miró, Martin Johnson Heade, John Ottis Adams, Gustav Klimt, Maria Van Oosterwyck, Rachel Ruysch, Ambrosius Bosschaert, Balthasar van der Ast, Jan van Huysum, Margaretha Haverman, Cy Twombly, Angie Lewin, David Hockney, Johann Adalbert Angermayer, Renoir, Degas, van Gogh, Monet, Cezanne, Graham Brown, Ruskin, Singer Sargent, Rilke, Mackintosh, Nerys Johnson, Arthur Harry Church, Giuseppe Castiglione, Odilon Redon, Macoto Murayama. You might also like to consider the depiction of flowers in Chinese, Japanese or Aboriginal art, or flowers in other mediums such as photography, textiles or ceramics – for example, Turkish tulip tiles.

> Variation: This could be an individual, pair or small group task. Working in pairs or small groups, give the children an artist or a painting to research and present to the class.

7   From their selection, the children must whittle down their choices to create their own top ten flower paintings. Ask them to research and write a mini-biography of their chosen artists, a critical response to the paintings (this could be an annotated version of the painting and/or a brief paragraph) and consider how the artists and the paintings fit in with the period of history in which they lived. This information could be presented in an attractive virtual gallery that is inviting and easy for people to follow.

> Note: If you opt for the 'bold extension' of a school floral art show, then you will need to do a ballot to vote for the class top ten from the children's collective choices. You will also need to begin the practical work described on page 126.

8   Finally, using van Gogh's *Sunflowers* as a primary influence, ask the children to recreate their own artistic floral arrangement. This could draw on van Gogh's other paintings or reflect on his life. Place this next to his painting and ask the children to discuss the differences.

Some things you might like to discuss

❀   Van Gogh's paintings, *Irises* and *Sunflowers*, broke sales records when they were sold in 1987: *Irises* sold for £27 million and *Vase with Fifteen Sunflowers* sold for £25 million. Why might they have sold for that much? What is your opinion of their worth?

Learning to go: Ask the children to paint a picture of a flower in the style of one of the top ten artists or one of their favourite artists. Get them to take a photo and add it to their virtual gallery or, if they are involved in the school floral art show, place it with the relevant painting and invite people to comment.

Extra English: Get the children to write a mini-biography of their chosen artist. Remind them to consider their style: who are they writing for? They should try to get the right balance between entertaining and informative. They could be really imaginative here and try out different styles and formats – for example, they could present the information in the form of a cartoon of the artist with speech bubbles giving information. Remind them to use the first person if they do this.

A fraction of maths: Look at the different types of auction styles that exist and hold your own school or class art auction using five of the paintings. Give each child a certain amount of currency to spend. They could even create their own currency – agreeing its worth in advance, of course. Add a few rules to spice things up a bit, such as deciding that only prime numbers may be used when bidding, or multiples of 7. Work out the differences in price at the end of the auction and rank the top five paintings in order of cost. Work out the average cost of the flower paintings.

Holocaust Symbolism[2]

The following lesson is a delicate way of approaching a very harrowing subject, and at the same time learning about the sophisticated concept of symbolism.

Main subjects covered

History	ICT
RE	Maths
PSHE	English

Resources

Rose Blanche by Ian McEwan, illustrated by Roberto Innocenti (Red Fox, 2004)
Primary and secondary sources showing the effects of the Second World War on people and places

Some useful words you might like to use

Bystander
Holocaust
Perpetrator
Primary source
Rescuer
Secondary source
Symbolism
Victim

2 This session was inspired by Andrew Wrenn, 'Examples of Practice: Rose Blanche', *Historical Association* (20 February, 2013). Available at: <http://www.history.org.uk/resources/secondary_resource_1140,1149_8.html>.

The session

1 Begin the session with a moral discussion. Show the children an evocative picture of someone in trouble, perhaps from a current world event, such as children fleeing from a bomb blast or natural disaster. You could ask the children a number of questions for them to discuss in pairs:

 ❀ What do they think is going on in the picture?

 ❀ Who is in trouble and why?

 ❀ What might the scene have looked like one minute/hour before and after?

 ❀ How does this image make you feel?

 ❀ What could be done to help the people in the picture?

 ❀ Would you help them? What might stop you from helping them? What might prompt you to help them?

 ❀ What if you were one of those people – what would you like someone to do to help you?

> **Variations:** This activity could be done as a whole-class discussion or you could give the children the questions before they see the picture and ask them to note down their ideas on a piece of sugar paper before presenting their ideas to the class.

2 Hopefully, the children can begin to see that morality is a complex issue, and that what we would like to do and what we actually do can be very different. Discuss what makes a person risk their own well-being for someone else, particularly for those they do not know. Discuss what could prompt a person to change from being a bystander to a rescuer.

> **Extension:** The children could research or be presented with people throughout history who have put their own lives at risk for others. Discuss the characteristics these people share and consider what the world would be like without such individuals.

3 Explain that during the Second World War lots of ordinary people helped friends and strangers who were in trouble because they were being persecuted by the Nazis. Tell the children that they are going to hear a story about a girl who makes a moral journey – moving from being a benign supporter of the Nazis and a bystander during events to helping those in need.

4 Introduce the story of *Rose Blanche*. Tell the children that you will read the story first without stopping – it is not very long. Make sure the children can see the pictures as you read.

5 After reading the story, ask the children if they have any questions they would like to ask about the story or the

pictures. Give them a few minutes to consider, perhaps talking it through with a group, partner or writing down a few questions. Discuss questions and possible answers as a whole class.

6   Before you reread the story for a second time, the previous activity should bring you neatly on to examining the historical ideas in *Rose Blanche*. Explain that the book is a secondary source – information provided after the event by someone who wasn't there at the time. They might also use primary sources to find out information – a primary source is a piece of contemporary material evidence created by someone who was there, such as letters or photographs.

7   Show the children a range of primary sources that Roberto Innocenti might have used to help him illustrate the book. You might like to display them next to relevant references in the story. You could consider pictures of the swastika, German and Russian soldiers, tanks and other vehicles, Hitler (the fat mayor is deliberately depicted to resemble him), the famous picture of the young boy in the Warsaw ghetto with his hands in the air (referenced in the story when the young boy escapes from the van only to be caught by the fat mayor and the SS guard), pictures of concentration camps and prisoners, the yellow 'Jude' star, people fleeing their homes at the end of the war and the Rose Blanche group.

8   Using the yellow 'Jude' star, briefly explore the notion of symbolism – what it is and why and how it is used. Ask the children to consider symbolism as you reread the story.

Symbolic ideas to look out for include colours, Rose's red ribbon, the weather, seasons, flowers, badges and characters.

9   Now, reread the story for a second time, this time stopping at each picture to examine and discuss it in detail.

Some generic questions you might like to use[3]

❀   What do you see?

❀   Do you see characters in different settings or always the same? What does the setting suggest about them, if anything?

❀   What colours are used and how?

❀   What symbols are there, how are they used and is there any repetition?

❀   How would you describe the light used by the illustrator – is it dark or light? Light can attract the reader's attention to a particular area, while shadow creates a sense of danger and mystery.

❀   Where is the characters' gaze? How does this impact on your reading of the book?

---

3   These questions were adapted from: <https://www.det.nsw.edu.au/eppcontent/glossary/app/resource/factsheet/4122.pdf>.

How does the size of the characters and objects compare to one another? What does their relative size suggest about the characters' status or situation in the book?

How are the characters placed? Where are they on the page in comparison to the others?

Are there any objects or items shown with the characters? What does this association suggest about them?

What does the characters' clothing suggest about them and how does it contribute to the meaning of the story?

What are the characters' expressions like? How are they significant? Do they change?

What do the characters' postures tell you about them?

What did you like/dislike about the book?

What is the most disturbing part of the story for you?

What was the most memorable part of the story?

What did you think of the ending?

Whose side are you on?

Whose side is the writer on?

Some specific questions you might like to use

Consider what happened to Rose's red ribbon. Why does she no longer wear it? How does the way she looks at the end of the story compare to how she is depicted at the beginning? Why and how has she changed?

What does 'Winter is coming' suggest? How does it make you feel about the future?

What do you think happened to Rose?

How did the picture of the flowers make you feel about what had happened? What does it suggest about the future? Do you agree?

Why do you think the author chose to tell the story from a child's point of view?

10 After you have reread and discussed ideas from the book, emphasise how symbolism can quickly and implicitly tell a story of its own.

11 Explain that the children are now going to continue this idea of symbolism as they represent the story of Rose Blanche and the Holocaust in their own floral arrangement. Six yellow flowers will be used to represent the six million Jews who were killed by the Nazis during the Second World War; a red ribbon hanging in the trees symbolises Rose Blanche and her rejection of the Nazi ethos; the white lily represents Rose Blanche's innocence; the prickly texture of the white eryngium suggests the discomfort of those in the concentration camps, as well as representing the barbed wire,

keeping the prisoners in and the rescuers out; and the mitsu-mata represents the winter wood that Rose walked through to reach those in the camp.

Some things you might like to discuss

✿ What do you think of people who do not help those in trouble?

✿ What motivates someone to help another person, particularly someone they do not know?

✿ Why do people persecute others?

✿ Is it worth putting your own safety at risk to help someone else?

Learning to go: Looking at their six yellow flowers, ask the children to investigate the Holocaust and the experience of Jews during the Second World War. They could also consider why the Jewish people have such a long history of persecution. Get them to use their findings to prepare an assembly to deliver to the whole school on Holocaust Memorial Day using their symbolic floral arrangement as the visual stimulus and springboard. Remind them to include their personal opinions about what they have discovered.

Extra English: To elicit quality responses during discussions it is recommended that a little synonym or vocabulary work is done either before or during this activity. For example, a typical response to the photo of the Jewish boy in the Warsaw ghetto might be 'I feel sad' or 'They are sad', when in fact the children are likely to be feeling a range of differing, conflicting and more precise emotions that could be explored. Such an emotive platform is ripe for the exploration of nuances of meaning.

A fraction of maths: The children have six yellow flowers to represent the six million Jews who were killed by the Nazis during the Holocaust. Ask them to find out how many people in total died in combat during the Second World War. How do the two numbers compare? Ask them to express these as a ratio, percentage and fraction. What are their thoughts about these figures?

Extension: The children could investigate and analyse other statistics for the Holocaust – for example, how many non-Jews were killed.

Killers and Cures

They may look beautiful, but some flowers are fatal! The children will learn all about the deadly capabilities of some plants and hear gruesome stories about their uses. But don't worry, they will also look at a few cures too.

Main subjects covered

Maths

History

Science

English

Resources

Sugar paper

Killer flower cards

Cure flower cards

Some useful words you might like to use

Apothecary

Assumptions

Conclude

Deduce

Diagnose

Evidence

Flowers

Herbs

Nosegay

Plague

Posy

Primary source

Remedy

Secondary source

Speculate

Symptom

Tussie-mussie

The session

1 Play the nursery rhyme 'Ring a Ring o' Roses' and ask the children what they actually know about the song. Explain how some historians think it might be about the Great Plague of 1665–1666 that swept across Europe. Tell them that they will be looking at some evidence to support this idea and that they will also learn what role herbs and flowers had in medicine at that time.

> Variations: Show appropriate pictures to accompany the different lines of the nursery rhyme as you play it to the class.

2 Show primary (if possible) and secondary source pictures of the Great Plague, which should include a depiction of a plague doctor (you will be discussing the purpose of his beak later on) and images of the herbs and flowers used in nosegays. In groups, ask the children to become history detectives, reporting back to the class on what they deduce about that moment in time from the evidence they have in front of them – for example, beliefs, social order and way of life. Discuss how far their deductions are speculative and conclusive. What other evidence might they need to make firmer assumptions? How far can they trust the evidence in front of them?

3 Tell the children about the purpose of the doctor's beak – how it was stuffed with herbs and sweet-scented flowers, since they believed that bad air was the cause of infection. To a certain extent, they were on to something, since foul smells are indicative of disease, although at the time there was no understanding of bacteria or germ theory, which appeared much later on. Introduce the idea of the tussie-mussie, nosegay or posy which were used by people at that time to ward off disease. Investigate what the ingredients of such a nosegay might be. Consider who could afford nosegays. What repercussions might the affordability of nosegays and posies have on the spread of disease?

4 Take this opportunity to look at a range of herbs that can cure. Working in small groups, give the children between five and ten herbs to investigate. What do they look like? What are their uses? Their history and traditions? What properties do they have? Where do they come from? When might a cure become a killer?

5 Next, ask the children to work in pairs. Give each pair a large piece of sugar paper and a set of killer flower and cure flower information cards and a corresponding set of photos. Each card should include the flower's name – both common and Latin – and how it kills or cures (see the examples below).

KILLER	CURE
Monkshood	**Lavender**
Aconitum napellus	*Lavandula angustifolia*
Touch it	**Touch it**
Nasty rash	Soothes insect bites, burns, cuts and spots
Swellings	
Eat it	**Eat it**
Burning tongue	Relieves headaches and sore throats
Being sick	Aids sleep and relaxation
Tummy ache	
Diarrhoea	
Paralysis	
Death!	

The following table provides a few ideas for plants you could use. You could also give the flower names to the children and ask them to create their own set of cards.

KILLERS	CURES
Deadly nightshade	Dandelion
Elderflower	Geranium
Foxglove	Lavender
Henbane	Pot marigold
Lily of the valley	Rosemary
Monkshood	Sweet violet

6 The children must place the cards on the sugar paper under the correct headings and match the appropriate picture with the information.

7 Now play the 'being an apothecary' game in which the children get to cure or diagnose symptoms by choosing the correct flower. Not only does this game reinforce the learning in point number 5, but it is also an opportunity for the children to learn about different parts of the body.

8   For the 'curing' section of the game, a patient might walk into the surgery with, say, a kidney problem. From a multiple choice selection, the 'apothecary' has to decide which of dandelion, geranium or henbane will cure the patient. Include a killer flower among the choices (in this case henbane) to make it really critical for the apothecary to choose the correct flower. Keep a tally for how many were killed and cured!

9   The 'diagnosing symptoms' section of the game runs along similar principles, only this time the apothecary has to try and identify what caused the symptoms from a multiple choice selection of flowers. For example, a patient walks into the surgery with dilated pupils and blurry vision. Have they eaten lavender, deadly nightshade or lily of the valley? Again, keep a tally of how many the children diagnose correctly.

> **Variations:** Points number 8 and 9 could be a whole-class activity using PowerPoint slides or it could be turned into a drama piece.

10 The children are now in a position to make their own medicinal tussie-mussie with the knowledge that it will cure and not kill!

Some things you might like to discuss

❁ What flowers are used in medicine today?

❁ What has this session taught you about the nature of flowers?

❁ How has your attitude to flowers and herbs been changed by this session?

❁ What surprised you most about the killer flowers?

❁ What flowers would you like to know more about?

> **Learning to go:** Encourage the children to grow their own cures by cultivating a medicinal herb garden. Suggest they have a cup of mint tea when they have finished, knowing it will do them good!
>
> **Extra English:** Ask the children to make their own 'A Little Guide to Killers and Cures' reference book aimed at children of their own age. They could include drawings and photos, the common and Latin names of plants, as well as showing how they kill and cure. The children could concentrate on plants and herbs that are native to their own country if they wish, or they could just focus on killers if they are feeling particularly gory!
>
> **A fraction of maths:** Using the results from their tally chart in point numbers 8 and 9, get the children to create a bar graph. They should then work out their percentage success rate. What was their success/failure ratio? Get them to determine how successful they were as an apothecary. They could also create a class database, finding out which questions people scored better and worst at – what were the percentages?

Let's Celebrate

Prepare the children to party in their very own Battle of the Flowers, while discovering the huge part flowers play in many different festivals, ceremonies and celebrations around the world.

Main subjects covered

Music
RE
PE: dance
Geography

MFL
Maths
English

Resources

Musical instruments and equipment
Photos
Music
Stories

Some useful words you might like to use

Carnival
Celebration
Ceremony
Culture
Festival
Ritual

The session

1   Show the children a selection of flowers, real or photographic, and discuss how flowers make them feel and what they signify for them.

> Variation: You could show them the flowers one by one, giving them time to observe and note down their emotional response to each flower. How does each flower affect them and why?

2   Follow this up by asking the children to discuss and write down what festivals, ceremonies and celebrations they know of in which flowers are used. Do they know how and why flowers are used in these particular events and what they might represent? If not, ask them to find out and share their research with the class, giving their thoughts about what they have learned as they go along.

3   Now, ask the children to consider how flowers are used as symbols in festivals, celebrations and ceremonies in other countries and cultures. You could either set this as a question and let the children find their own paths of discovery or you could direct them to specific ceremonies, celebrations, cultures and countries. Some ideas you could use include: Loi Kratong (Buddhism: Thailand, Laos, Burma), Teacher's Day (Thailand), Valentine's Day (worldwide), Quinceañera (Central/South America), Lei and Tiare (Tahiti), Flower Gazing (Taoism), Onam, Diwali and Pongal (Hindu: India), May Day (pagan: northern hemisphere), Day of the Dead (Mexico), Almond Blossom Festival and Rose Festival

(Morocco). What have they learned? What comparisons can be made, if any, between the different festivals, celebrations and ceremonies they have found out about?

4   Once the children have compiled their list, find the countries on a map and highlight where the festivals take place (this would work well as part of a huge classroom display). You could also create a calendar of events to add to the display, identifying when the celebrations occur.

5   Ask the children to dig deeper and uncover what they can about one or two ceremonies, celebrations or festivals. Split the class into small groups or pairs. Allocate the following research questions to different groups so that each group has an audience to enjoy the fruits of their research:

❀   Why are flowers used and what do they symbolise?

❀   What is the history or background of the festival, celebration or ceremony?

❀   What do the events mean to the people of that culture or country?

❀   What stories, music and dance are associated with the event?

❀   How do the events affect those involved?

❀   What do the rituals reveal or suggest about the country or culture?

🌸 How are the cultural celebrations similar or different from one another?

🌸 What is most interesting or fascinating about the event?

🌸 How do the beliefs of that culture differ from your own?

The children should present their findings to the class in any medium they wish.

6 Carnival time! Tell the children that they are now going to focus on the four-day Barranquilla Carnival in Colombia – the second biggest carnival in the world after Rio de Janeiro's Mardi Gras – with a mind to holding their own mini-carnival at your school. Present the children with photos, video and facts about the carnival or ask them to discover more themselves. What facts can they find out about the Battle of the Flowers? When does it take place? What is its history and origins? What cultural influences have an effect on the carnival? Get the children to listen to some of its musical genres (e.g. cumbia, puya, porro) and perhaps play some of the instruments (e.g. tambora and allegra drums, maracas, claves), watch the different dances (e.g. mico y micas, congo and palotea) and unearth and read associated folk stories. They could even learn some of the Spanish language associated with the carnival. There is plenty of information on the internet, so they should explore to really get to grips with it.

Extension: You could take this further by asking the children to find out what they can about Barranquilla and Colombia. What is the population? How do the people live? What is the land like? What type of climate does it have? What are its industries? How literate are the people?

7 Explain to the children that they are now going to prepare for their own Battle of the Flowers. To do this, they will be making a queen or king floral mask to wear. Give the children (old) flowers to do battle with (that is, throwing petals, not bashing one another over the heads with them!) and ask them to create their own music using traditional or non-traditional sounds. It doesn't stop there! Get the children to write poetry or 'traditional tales' to recite and include a choreographed dance. There is a lot to think about and organise, but it could be stunning – and fun!

Some things you might like to discuss

✿ Why do people have rituals and beliefs?

✿ Why do you think it is important for people to celebrate ideas and beliefs?

✿ How do festivals, celebrations and ceremonies enrich our lives, or don't they?

✿ Why do beliefs differ around the world?

✿ What do the different beliefs suggest about humans?

✿ Do you think there should be just one belief or is there room for lots?

Learning to go: As the children will have encountered during your research, different flowers have different meanings for particular countries and cultures. Invite them to do more research on the language of flowers and create their own 'Language of Flowers' dictionary. They could even try sending someone a secret message in flower code!

Extra English: The Barranquilla Carnival was declared a Masterpiece of the Oral and Intangible Heritage of Humanity by UNESCO in 2003, thereby preserving its traditional oral storytelling, dancing and music. Look at the rest of UNESCO's List of Intangible Cultural Heritage in Need of Urgent Safeguarding and Register of Good Safeguarding Practices. Ask the children to write their own flower-related folktale that they would like to have considered by UNESCO.

A fraction of maths: Organise and hold a 'Maths in Flowers' festival day at your school where all the maths problems and activities are related to flowers and plants. It could include Fibonacci numbers, symmetry and two- and three-dimensional shapes.

Peace in Our Time

The politicians declare that the war has ended, the soldiers have stopped fighting and the media rejoices … but then what? Using the end of the Second World War and the emergence of the United Nations as a focal stimulus, the children will explore the fallout of war and the charities that were set up to help those affected by it.

Main subjects covered

History	Maths
Geography	English

Resources

Children of Europe by David Seymour (UNESCO, 1949)

The Silver Sword by Ian Serraillier (Jonathan Cape, 1956) (specifically Chapter 11)

Some useful words you might like to use

Charity	Intellectual
Conflict	Organisation
Dispersed	Refugee
Dispossessed	Symbolism
Emblem	

The session

1   Pose the question, 'What happens after a war ends?', and discuss.

2   Show the children photos taken by David Seymour for UNESCO's *Children of Europe* (1949) publication. A PDF of the book is available at http://davidseymour.com/children-of-europe-paris-france-unesco-1949/, where you will also find an informative video (although it is perhaps a little slow and long to show in its entirety to some children).

3   Ask the children to note down their responses to the photographs using prompts such as:

❀   What has happened?

❀   How might the people in the photographs be feeling?

❀   How do you imagine their day-to-day existence?

❀   What do you think they will do next?

❀   Describe how you would respond in this situation.

❀   How might they be helped?

❀   How might you begin to rebuild a city/community? What do you think would be needed? What difficulties might you encounter?

❀   Is there anything that surprises you about the photographs?

❀   Explain which was the most shocking or moving photograph for you.

4   Now move on to a piece of text. Introduce the story of *The Silver Sword* by Ian Serraillier. If you are not familiar with it, it is the moving story of a Polish family who are torn apart by war. Separated and dispersed, the narrative chronicles the children's hazardous journey across post-war Europe in the hope they may once again be reunited with their parents. A dispossessed boy called Jan, a tragic figure whose life has been destroyed by war in many ways, travels with them.

5   Quickly summarise chapters 1 to 10, then read Chapter 11, 'The Road to Posen', together. As you are reading the chapter, show some photographs that will bring to life some of the descriptive post-war detail of the book. This will also help the children to visualise this very different world. For example, find pictures that show a city or street in ruins; a road crowded with refugees; the debris of war – derelict tanks, shell cases, dugouts, twists of barbed wire; barracks; and Red Cross camps. Look at a map of Europe and find Warsaw, Posen and the area of Appenzell, Switzerland. Chapter 11 sees the characters walk from Warsaw to Posen. They are aiming to get to Switzerland. Discuss with the children whether they think Ruth, Edek, Bronia and Jan will finish the journey or not. What might stop them? To find out if they make it or not, the children will have to read the rest of the book!

6   After reading the chapter, sort the children into groups, giving each group a selection of the following questions and activities based around what they have read:

❀ What do you think of the man's attitude in the last paragraph? Why do you think he felt that way? What would you have done in his position?

❀ How do you think Ruth felt on hearing the news that her brother had run away that morning?

❀ What do you think has happened to Jimpy? Why might Jan be so attached to the cockerel?

❀ Look at the language in the first paragraph. What words suggest hope? Does this mean that they will be successful?

❀ Why do you think the opening begins so positively? How does it compare with the end of the chapter? Why do you think the author decided to structure the chapter in this way?

❀ Underline any words in the chapter that tell you something about the environment. What are your impressions of the post-war setting?

❀ Edek has tuberculosis and receives no medical attention. What is TB and what do you think will happen to him?

❀ How do you feel about Ruth and her situation at the end of the chapter?

❀ Underline words and phrases that tell you something about Ruth. How is she presented? Do you like her? Does she remind you of anyone?

❀ What have you learned from reading this chapter?

❀ How are the barracks presented?

❀ Look at the words used to describe Warthe camp. How is it presented?

❀ In the last paragraph the man sounds 'weary and bitter' – why?

❀ Have you ever felt like any of the characters?

❀ How effective is the ending of the chapter? Why do you think the author chose to end it like this?

❀ What do you think the future holds for the children?

❀ How do you think the writer feels about the effects of war? Who does he sympathise with?

❀ Why do you think the writer spends time describing the settings?

7 The children should now have a good grasp of some of the post-war effects on people and the landscape. Explain that while civilians 'on the ground' were trying to survive and cope, politicians from many countries were also trying to find a way forward so that war might never happen again. One way they did this was by forming the United Nations in 1945, and its 'intellectual' arm, UNESCO, whose mission is to build lasting peace and security. UNESCO believes that lasting peace depends on how men and women ultimately think and what their attitudes are, and therefore it concentrates on influencing education, science and culture.

8 Ask the children to find out what they can about the United Nations, UNESCO and UNICEF. What do the children think of their main goals? Discuss the United Nations Convention on the Rights of the Child. Get the children to design posters around these rights, including a selection of flowers to symbolise each right.

Extension: Look at the roles charities play in helping those who have been affected by war, or those charities that are helping to bring about peace. You could ask the children to find their own or you could direct them to specific websites, such as UNICEF, War Child or Children of Peace. Ask the children to consider what the word 'charity' means to them. What role do charities have in helping those who have been affected by war? Are there too many charities? Have the children ever given to charity or been charitable? What is the history of charity? What would a world without charity look like?

9 Ask the children to look at the United Nations emblem. How well does this represent the organisation? Now begin to explore the idea of peace symbolism. The UN emblem includes an olive branch, which is an ancient symbol of peace originating in Greece. Ask the children to find out about other plants that have been used to symbolise peace or movements associated with peace. Some ideas to consider include: the lotus flower in Asia; the red poppy as a symbol of remembrance with an associated desire that war should not happen again; White Rose was the name of a Second World War German resistance group; a peace rose was given to each of the delegates at the inaugural UN meeting in 1945; flower power was a symbol of passive resistance to the Vietnam War in the 1960s; and the Battle of the Flowers in Barranquilla was originally organised to replace the bullets of war with flowers of peace.

10 Finally, ask the children to consider what colours they associate with peace.

11 The children are now ready to design their own peace wreath using the colours, flowers and symbols discussed.

Note: You could use the peace wreath as an emblem for your own peace organisation or charity.

Some things you might like to discuss

✿ How do you think the world will finally find peace?

✿ Explore how possible a peaceful world is.

✿ Has the world become more or less peaceful since the Second World War? Give reasons for your ideas.

✿ What role can you play in making the world more peaceful?

✿ Why are flowers used as a symbol to promote peace?

Learning to go: Ask the children to find out where modern wars are going on today. Encourage them to research the background of these conflicts – for example, how long have they been going on? Who are the warring parties? How many people have lost their lives? What actions has the United Nations taken? What is the economic and educational impact? Then ask them to write a letter to an imaginary child who is caught up in a conflict, offering them support and including a pressed flower arrangement as a symbol of their friendship and hope for the future.

Extra English: Get the children to imagine they are a member of a newly created charity and they are debating which flower should be their emblem. They must choose a flower they like and try to persuade the others in their group why their flower should be the emblem.

A fraction of maths: Ask the children to choose one country (which should be a member of the United Nations) from each continent. Ask them to find out what the national flower of these countries is and to use this in their key as a symbol to represent population numbers. The children should decide how many people they want to equal one flower. Ask them to calculate how many flower symbols they will need to represent the population of each country. Get them to display their data as an infographic using three different methods of data presentation. What questions would they like to ask about their findings?

Staying Alive

The children will take a look at how plants grow and discover why, if you are running a successful floristry business, understanding, appreciating and applying a little bit of this scientific knowledge could help a business to bloom rather than wilt.

Main subjects covered

Science
Maths

English

Resources

Flowers
Foliage
Microscope

Some useful words you might like to use

Angle	Humidity
Applications	Hydrotropism
Botany	Osmosis
Cell	Photosynthesis
Chloroplast	Phototropism
Classification	Respiration
Degree	Stomata
Energy	Temperature
Equations	Thigmotropism
Geotropism	Transpiration

The session

1   Give the children the 'Useful words you might like to use' list that, as a good florist, they would be expected to know and understand.

2   Ask the children to sort the words into four groups: (a) what they definitely know about, (b) what they think they know about, (c) what they would like to have a guess at and (d) what they really have no idea about. The prefixes or suffixes of some of the words will hopefully give them some clues. Discuss the results.

> **Variation:** This could be done individually, in small groups or as a whole class using an interactive whiteboard.

3   Tell the children that, for the purposes of this session, you will be focusing on photosynthesis, transpiration and phototropism.

> **Variation:** If you wish to concentrate solely on one aspect that is fine, as is looking at any of the other terms in the list above.

4   Show the children a plant and tell them that plants, like humans, need food to grow. Ask them to examine their flowers or plants and see if they can see any hands or mouths. Obviously, the answer will be no, so how do plants 'eat'?

5   Introduce the idea that plants make most of the food they need through their leaves using photosynthesis. At this point, you could ask them to take a closer look at the leaves and tell you what they see, speculating on how this could happen. Perhaps they might like to note down their ideas which they can amend as more information is revealed.

6   Show them the mnemonic SAW (Sunlight, Air, Water) and explain that these are the three ingredients needed by plants to make food. Ask them to revisit their ideas or notes from point number 5 and get them to revise them or speculate once more.

7   Begin to explain the role of the three ingredients: leaves catch the sunlight; leaf openings called stomata (a great word!) let in carbon dioxide from the air and let out oxygen; plant roots absorb water from the soil and, in turn, leaves draw water up the stem from the roots – this last action is called osmosis.

> **Variation:** To help the children remember stomata, ask them to say 'tomato' out loud. Then ask them to shout out the word again, but put an 's' in front. They will enjoy this and feel very intelligent knowing they can say such a scientific word!
>
> You could ask the children if they can see the stomata in the leaves. Some will say they can, at which point you can commend them on how amazing that is! You could then get out a microscope and ask them to draw and describe the differences in what they can see with the instrument and what they can see with the naked eye.

You could use the microscope activity to springboard into the history of how and what people have used over time to observe and study science. For example, when was the microscope invented and by whom? What needed to be invented or understood before this step could take place?

You could go on to look at the root systems of plants and consider how and why they differ.

8 Hold up a leaf and tell the children how sunlight, air and water are mixed together in the chloroplasts (the part of the leaf cell that catches the sun's energy), resulting in the production of sugar (the plant food – yum, yum!) and oxygen (the chemical by-product of the mixing).

9 Show the children a real flower stem or a picture of a bunch of flowers and ask them, 'So how does all this apply to floristry?' Explain that when the flower is cut away from the main plant it begins to die, but the speed at which it dies can be reduced by the florist if they understand the three food needs of a plant – SAW.

10 Time for a little water experiment. Each child will need four cut flowers of the same type, but try to have range of different flowers spread among the class to evaluate the various 'strengths' of each of the flowers. For example, child A could have four carnations, while child B could have four roses. Remove as many of the leaves from each flower stem as possible because trying to feed the leaves and the flower will take up too much energy. In floristry, this is called conditioning. In your experiment, treat each flower as follows:

Flower 1: Leave out of water.

Flower 2: Cut the stem at a 45 degree angle and place in clean water. Do not change the water during the experiment.

Flower 3: Cut the stem at a 45 degree angle and place in fresh water every day.

Flower 4: Cut the stem at a 45 degree angle and place in clean water with flower food, repeating all three actions daily.

11 Ask the children to keep a record, noting down what they notice at three intervals during the day. This could be first thing in the morning, lunchtime and at the end of school. What changes do they notice in the petals, stem and water? Which flower lasts longest? How did the different types of flowers compare? What can they conclude from the experiment? What advice would they now give to someone who bought cut flowers if they wanted them to last as long as possible?

Variation: You could conduct a similar experiment without removing the leaves from the stems and record what occurs. Are there any differences in flower longevity with or without leaves?

NB: Take care with your choices of flower because some flowers, believe it or not, do not like flower food!

12 Explain that florists use flower food as a substitute for the sugar the flower would normally make itself. Cutting the stems at a 45 degree angle gives the stem a greater surface

area from which to suck up water. Cut stems can heal over, inhibiting any further water intake, so it is important to recut the stems from time to time. As a florist, you want the flowers to live and look good for as long as possible. No one wants to be a sad, brown, drooping flower! What would happen to your business?

13 Moving on from photosynthesis, a successful florist really needs to be mindful of transpiration. Explain that transpiration is the loss of water from a flower through its leaves, stems or petals. Light, temperature, wind and humidity are the four factors that affect transpiration.

14 Experiment time again, this time looking at light and temperature. Each child could have two flowers, both of which are treated as flower 3 above. Place one flower by a sunny windowsill and one in a cool, dark place. The children should record what happens to each flower over the period of a week. Which lasts the longest? What do the children conclude?

Variation: You could repeat the experiment, but mist the flowers this time and see how this affects the previous results. Note, for a more reliable result make sure you use the same type of flower as you did for point number 14.

If you wanted to look at humidity, you could place both flowers on a sunny windowsill and mist one and not the other.

If you wanted to consider wind, place one of the flowers in a draughty place and the other away from a draught. For reliable results, try to keep all the other factors constant. Alternatively, talk about the effects of wind on clothes hanging on a washing line.

The results should look something like this:

Factors effecting transpiration		Result
Light	Bright light	Fast
Wind	Windy conditions	Fast
Temperature	High temperature	Fast
Humidity	Humid conditions	Slow

In general, flowers open quicker in light and warmth, but last longer in indirect light and cooler temperatures.

15 Finally, introduce the final term for this session – phototropism. Explain to the children that this is when a flower stem bends towards the light. Again, you could conduct an experiment here with two flowers, placing one flower on a sunny windowsill and the second in the same room, but away from the window. How long does it take for the stem to bend towards the light? Why would you need to consider phototropism as a florist?

16 Tell the children that they are now going to put all their scientific experimentation and learning into practice and answer a few floristry conundrums. This is a fun activity to end the session. When considering a response, ask them to consider WALT (Water, Air, Light and Temperature). Working in small groups, show the children some floristry problems with multiple choice answers. They then have to decide which is the correct answer and why.

❀ You have a wedding in three days' time and the flowers have not opened yet. What will you do?

   a   Panic!

   b   Cut the stems, put them in water and place in a sunny spot.

   c   Put them in a cold, dark place.

❀ You have made buttonholes the day before the wedding. What will you do to keep them looking good for the big day?

   a   Put them in a really warm, light place.

   b   Put them in a cool, dark place and mist regularly.

   c   Put them in the freezer.

❀ You have just opened a floristry shop. Where will you display your flowers?

   a   In the sunny, warm window.

   b   Next to the shaded till.

   c   Outside by the doorway.

❀ What are the advantages and disadvantages of all three of these choices? Which flowers would cope better in each spot?

> **Variation:** You could do this quiz as a whole class, or you could dispense with the multiple choice answers and just show the questions.

17 Finally, get the children to design their own art arrangement that highlights their understanding of the science of flowers in floristry, and ask them to explain how they would look after it so that it lasts as long as possible.

Some things you might like to discuss

❀ Were you surprised by anything in this session?

❀ Why experiment?

❀ Are there any reasons why we use Greek and Latin terminology in science, and specifically with plants?

Learning to go: Inquisitive and creative scientists like to see how they can use their knowledge and understanding of how things work and live to investigate potential alternative uses. The applications of photosynthesis include creating new artificial energy, capturing oxygen, detecting and treating cancerous tumours, creating artificial sight, increasing crop yields and developing computer electronics. Discuss these ideas with the children – which are they most amazed or surprised by? Ask them to investigate any of these ideas further and report back their findings to the class. To add a little bit of humour to the whole process, they could even dress up as stereotypical scientists when they deliver their findings!

Extra English: Encourage the children to learn a little Latin or Greek as they investigate the meanings of the prefixes and suffixes in this session. For example, what does the word 'tropism' mean? Ask them to find out what phototropism, geotropism, hydrotropism and thigmotropism are. What do the prefixes 'photo', 'geo', 'hydro' and 'thigmo' mean? Which language do they come from? What other words can they think of that begin with these prefixes? Which are Latin and which are Greek? Can they see any differences between when Latin is used rather than Greek, or vice versa? Get the children to create a permanent illustrated class 'prefix and suffix' display showing origins and definitions. Keep adding to it throughout the year.

Afterwards, ask the children to find different flowers or plants that show each of the four different tropisms. Get them to draw or download pictures and label them. Now ask them to imagine they are a villainous top scientist and they want to rule the world. They will do this by creating a new plant super-breed using one of the tropisms to give it its strength. When they have created their flower monster, get the children to record a message to play to the world detailing just how they intend to conquer it! Or maybe read John Wyndham's *The Day of the Triffids* instead!

A fraction of maths: Get the children to write an equation to show photosynthesis. Don't forget to explain what an equation is if the children are not familiar with the term. Some examples might include: light + air + water = sugar; sun + carbon dioxide + water = food + oxygen; or my personal favourite that one pupil came up with: sunshine + air + water = life. The equations could be used as part of a display.

The Birds and the Bees

How does a flower go forth and multiply? What are the rules of attraction? And what exactly do birds and bees have to do with it? All will be revealed!

Main subjects covered

Science – life processes, living things

Maths

English

Resources

Flowers or plants

Fruit (e.g. apples, sycamore 'wings', nuts, berries, poppy heads, pea pods)

Images showing the parts of a flower

Microscopes

Magnifying glasses

Recording devices

Toy bee or butterfly

Some useful words you might like to use

Anther	Petal
Botany	Pistil
Calyx	Pollination
Corolla	Reproduction
Dispersal	Sepal
Fertilisation	Stamen
Filament	Stigma
Germination	Style
Ovary	Symbiosis
Pedicel	

The session

1   Begin by creating a great fuss with the children over the idea that they are going to become professional botanists. They will be looking closely at the parts of a real flower using microscopes, learning the role of each part of the flower and using the language of the experts. They will then create a flower arrangement that will show all stages of the growth process.

2   Give each child a flower of their own and ask them, first of all, to look carefully at the flower and note down what they notice about it. You may get responses along the lines of its colour as well as being able to name the petals, leaf and stem. You may want to prompt them as to the flower's texture, strength, size, quantity of leaves or number of flowers on a stem. Explain that all of these features have a purpose or role in the flower's continuing survival – something they will look at in more depth later in this session.

> **Note and extension:** The children don't all have to have the same flowers. In fact, I would encourage you to use a range of flowers so that you can begin to look at classification: what do all flowers have in common? How do they differ? Why might they differ? Ask the children to find out about their original habitat and consider how this might affect their form.

3   Next, show the children a labelled picture of a bisected flower highlighting, for example, the stamen, pistil, sepal and pedicel. Read out the words together so that the children are secure as to their pronunciation.

Be an expert: use the language.

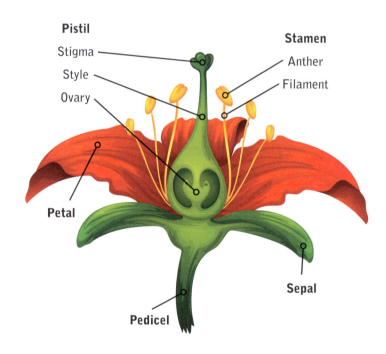

Botany of a flower

4   Explain that you are all going to look at these flower parts in closer detail, and like all serious student botanists, remind them that it is a good idea to take notes as they go along.

> Variation: You could give children free reign on note-taking or provide them with an organised task sheet.

5   Now show the children a series of images focusing on each of the main flower parts. After each picture, invite the children to return to their real flowers and identify the part of the flower shown in the image. Then ask them what role they think this part of a flower might have. You may want to reassure them that you are not necessarily expecting a 'correct' answer, but a logical one. The point is to try and stimulate their curiosity about the make-up of a flower.

6   After you have talked about the attractiveness of the colour of the petals to different insects, begin to explain to the children that the aim of all living things is to reproduce, to make again (from the Latin *re*, which means 'again' or 'anew', and produce, which means to 'bring forth' or 'extend'), and that plants have lots of cunning ways of reproducing – the colour of their petals being just one of them. Explain that some flowers need the help of insects and birds to help them reproduce, and you are now going to find out why.

7   Tell the children that a flower has a male and female part. Explain that the male part of a flower is called the stamen, which is easy to remember because it has the word 'men' in its name. Ask the children to carefully remove the petals to expose the stamen in their flower and to look at the stamen using a magnifying glass. What do they notice? Then ask them to look for the anther and filament and explain their roles in the reproductive process. Invite the children to remove the stamen and examine it under a microscope. What do they see? Can they see any pollen on the anther?

> Extension: As the children remove different parts of the flower they could stick them on to a sheet, label them and display it.

8   Now show an image of the female part of the flower, the pistil, and, using a magnifying glass, once again invite the children to identify the stigma, style and ovary. Ask them to remove the pistil and look at it under a microscope. How would they describe what they see? Explain the roles of each part.

> Note: You will need to bisect the flower to see the ovary.

9   Explain that a plant reproduces by making seeds. For a flower to make a seed it must be pollinated – that is, pollen from the male anther must touch the female stigma of another flower (you may want to look again at the stamen under a microscope or magnifying glass here). When this happens pollination has taken place, the ovules become fertilised and eventually they turn into seeds. Invite the children to consider how a flower manages to pollinate another flower if it cannot get up out of the ground and move.

10 Before moving on to pollination, you might like to recap on some of the botanical terms you have covered. Ask the children to create a mnemonic to help them remember these wonderful words. Tell them that you are going to quickly test their botanical knowledge – show them a picture of the flower again but without the labels. Can the children identify each part of the flower?

11 Now you can begin discussing the next stage in the life cycle of a plant: pollination. Explain that plants rely mostly on insects to pollinate them – they have a symbiotic (from the Greek meaning 'living together') relationship, which means they need one another to survive. Demonstrate how this happens using real flowers and a toy bee or butterfly and, for reinforcement, ask the children to dramatise the process. One way of dramatising this might be to have one child as a bee, two groups of children representing two flowers each of which has one girl (the pistil) at the centre of a circle of boys (the stamen). The 'bee' could buzz around one 'flower', pick up some pollen from the boys and 'fly over' to other flower, placing the pollen on the girl's head!

Extension: You could talk about the insect 'landing strip' or nectar guides that flowers helpfully display to further their chances of pollination – some we can see and others only insects can see. How else might a flower attract pollinators? Ask the children to find out what other pollinating insects or mammals there are other than butterflies and bees. They will be amazed! Find out what flowers attract a particular insect, bird or mammal and how. Why might a plant do this? What are the advantages and disadvantages of this rule of attraction?

12 Explain that another method of pollination is wind, used mainly by trees and grasses, our oldest 'flowers'. What do they think might be the advantages and disadvantages of this method? The flower does not have to rely on insects for survival, but while a lot of pollen is produced, a lot is wasted.

13 Next, show the children a range of fruits and explain that after pollination the flower's job is done. The petals fall away and the ovary becomes a fruit that contains one or more seeds – the potential beginnings of another plant where the hard outer layer contains an embryo (a baby plant) and stored food. The range of fruit displayed could be those we typically see as 'fruit', such as oranges, lemons or apples, but also show sycamore 'wings', hips, haws, berries, nuts, poppy heads, burrs and bean or pea pods, all of which offer scope for discussion. Open up the fruits to reveal the seeds and get the children using magnifying glasses and microscopes. What similarities and differences are there?

14 After the children have examined the different types of fruit and seed, describe the various methods of seed dispersal – wind, water, animals and birds, self-dispersal (e.g. explosion) – and ask the children to consider which ones might be used in the dispersal of the seeds they have in front of them. How might each one scatter its seeds? Which methods of dispersal are more or less reliable? What are the advantages and disadvantages of each method? Explain that the job of the fruit is to carry the seed as far away as it can from its parent plant, so that there is no competition for light, water and soil-based food or nutrients.

> Extension: Once again, you could include a classification exercise here – size, shape, weight and quantity of seed. How might these attributes influence dispersal? If a flower, for example a poppy, produces lots of small, light seeds, what can the children conclude about the flower? It generally doesn't live very long, therefore it needs to produce many 'youngsters' to guarantee continuance. It wants its seeds to be dispersed by the wind over a great distance, but its chances of successful dispersal are negligible if it produces so many seeds. How might this compare with a fruit that produces only one seed? How does the potential life span of that plant contrast to that of a poppy?

15 Finally, consider the final step of a flower's life cycle: germination. Discuss how, after the seed has dispersed, it may well find itself in the conditions it needs to grow, for the embryo to break free from the hard outer casing, producing an underground root and an above-ground shoot. Working in groups, give the children a paper plate, cotton wool and some mustard seeds. Ask them to dampen the cotton wool and, following the instructions on the seed packet, sow the seeds and check each day at regular intervals for signs of germination. The children could record their observations using a camera or through illustrations, noting the date and time as they go. Consider what emerges first, the root or the shoot? Why does the root emerge first? Why are the first two leaves that grow from the seed different to the leaves that subsequently appear?

> Variation and extension: The children could experiment with the conditions that a seed needs to germinate – that is, warmth, water and oxygen. They could place cuttings (e.g. willow stems) in a water-filled test tube and examine them for root formation. They could then discuss the differences between creating plants through cuttings rather than seeds. A seed will be an individual plant that may differ slightly to its parent, whereas a cutting will be a clone of its parent.

16 The children should finish off by creating their own floral arrangements that highlight the different stages of a flower's life cycle.

Some things you might like to discuss

❀ What is the point of reproduction?

❀ Why is it important to understand the way a plant reproduces?

❀ Why is it helpful to know the botanical names of parts of a flower?

❀ How is pollination important to humans?

❀ What insect is most vital to humans' continuing existence?

❀ What plant is most vital to humans' continuing existence?

❀ Can humans live without plants?

Learning to go: Ask the children to make recycled plant pots or paper pots, fill them with seed compost and germinate a selection of seeds. Get them to watch and record their growth, caring and tending to their every need. When the seedlings are big enough and the weather is sufficiently warm (usually around May), ask them to plant the seedlings in their paper pots in their garden at home or school. Remind the children to water them well when they plant them out and let nature do the rest. Finally, encourage them to enjoy the beauty of the flower they have helped to grow.

Extra English: It's all Greek to me! Get the children to find out the word origins of the botanical terms they have learned. Which words are of Greek origin and which of Latin? How apt are the botanical names?

Here are some examples.

Greek		Latin	
Calyx/Sepal – covering	Petal – thin plate	Corolla – little crown	Stamen – thread
Anther – flower	Perianth – around the flower	Pistil – pestle	Style – stylus
Stigma – spot		Ovary – egg	

A fraction of maths: Ask the children to look at their woodland wall hanging and identify any shapes they can see. What is the most common shape? How many triangles are there in their design? Can they name the different types? What are the angles within the shapes? What is the proportion of acute angles as opposed to obtuse angles? Now ask them to consider measurements. What is the width and length of their design? What is the circumference and area?

Where the Wild Things Are

Maps at the ready as the children find out what wild plants grow where and why in their country and around the world.

Main subjects covered

Science

Geography

Art

Maths

English

Resources

Where the Wild Things Are by Maurice Sendak (Harper & Row, 1963)

Sugar paper

Felt-tip pens or crayons

Maps

Flower cards

Some useful words you might like to use

Beach	Mountain
Biomes	Ocean
Cliff	River
Climate	Savannah
Coast	Sea
Desert	Season
Diversity	Soil
Environment	Tundra
Flora	Valley
Forest	Vegetation
Habitat	Vegetation belts
Hill	Weather
Landscape	Wood

The session

1   Introduce the idea of habitat by reading *Where the Wild Things Are* by Maurice Sendak. Although aimed at young children, it has much worth for older children either to rediscover or to meet for the first time. There are lots of questions you could ask the children about the illustrations, characters, framing and symbolism, but for the benefit of this session we will be focusing on the setting, or habitat. Questions you might like to ask the children include:

❀   What habitat is being depicted?

❀   What plants would you expect to see growing there and why?

❀   Why did Sendak choose this habitat for Max to meet the wild things?

❀   What habitat would you journey to if you wanted to feel free?

❀   How does the habitat make you feel? Would you like to go there?

❀   What words would you use to describe the habitat?

❀   What else might you expect to find in the place where the wild things live (e.g. animals, geographical and physical features)?

2   Explain to the children that a habitat is an environment where animals or plants live. Weather, soil, water, heat and light decide what plants will live where. There are many different habitats around the world.

3   Explore some of the features of different habitats by showing the children pictures of various types and, using weather, soil, water, heat and light as your headings, ask them to discuss or note down what they think the features of each habitat might be. For example, what would the weather be like in a desert? What is the soil like (if any)? How much water would there be? Use a map to locate some of the habitats.

> **Variation:** Ask the children to match pictures of habitats with an appropriate descriptor. The exploration of habitats could be micro or macro – for example, you could consider the different habitats in your own area or country, or you could show the class a natural vegetation world map and consider global differences instead.

4   Ask the children if they know any habitats like these? Have they ever been to any of these habitats? If so, invite them to tell the class about their experiences. What did they notice? How did it differ to other habitats they have experienced? What plants, trees, insects and animals might they expect to find in these diverse habitats? How are they able to survive? How are these different living things classified and why?

5   In groups of three, ask the children to draw a map of a pretend island that has a range of physical features – for example, a beach, river, woodland, mountains, lakes, prairie and rainforest. Don't forget to include a key!

6   Organise the children into small groups and hand out a set of flower cards (see the following examples) that highlight the particular conditions that each plant prefers, and perhaps indicating conditions they don't like.

Armeria maritima	Centaurea cyanus
Hello, my name is Thrift.	Hello, I am the lovely Cornflower.
I need sunshine and rain, but I cannot stand wet feet!	I love the sun.
I like to tuck into rocks and sand.	You sometimes see me growing with grass.
I am very strong and brave and will not let the wind bully me!	I like being in the open.

7   Using the clues on the flower cards, ask the children to place or stick the flower next to the appropriate habitat on the map. Other flowers you could consider include primrose, sea campion, yellow iris, ragged robin, purple loosestrife, poppy, bluebell, honeysuckle, wild garlic, starry saxifrage and moss campion – all of these plants have particular habitat needs! However, there are lots more plants out there in many locations that you could choose from.

Variation: Give the children plant names and ask them to research their particular habitat needs. Use grid references to pinpoint the flowers on a map.

8 Join the small working groups into bigger groups, say put two groups together, and let them compare their ideas. Do they want to make any changes as a result of their discussions?

9 Consider what other organisms, insects and animals they might find in these different habitats. How do they benefit the flowers?

10 Finally, using the habitat in *Where the Wild Things Are* as their inspiration, ask the children to create their own habitat floral arrangement, including flowers that enjoy similar growing conditions.

Some things you might like to discuss

❀ What habitats are you not likely to find in your country or local area? Why is this?

❀ How would you describe the habitat around your school or where you live?

❀ Describe what you think is the most interesting habitat and why.

Learning to go: Ask the children to identify what wild flowers grow near to where they live. Get them to begin making a wonderful floral logbook, including a pictorial record using their own drawings and photos. Ask them to find out what they can about each flower including any folklore, associations or symbolism.

Extra English: Invite the children to imagine that they are a plant hunter and they have discovered a new flower. Get them to write their diary entry for that evening, describing their joy and detailing what the plant looks like, the habitat they found it in and the conditions it will need to survive once a sample has been transported back to their own country. Get them to give their new flower a name and draw or 'take photos' of it. They could dress up as a plant hunter and utilise the school's green screen for this, if you have one!

A fraction of maths: Engage in some floral data collecting – the children could include this in their floral logbook. How many of the different wild flowers have they spotted near to where they live? Which flower appears most and which the least? Can they think of any reason for this? Copy the experts and choose a metre square area to study.

A Career in Floristry

Florists don't just work in shops (although it may be a good starting point to develop your skills). There are wonderful careers to be had with a floristry qualification – and it helps to know the maths.

Main subjects covered

English	ICT
PSHE	Maths
Art and design	

Resources

Floristry magazines and books
Qualities, skills and interests cards

Some useful words you might like to use

Calculation
Floristry
Interests
Metaphors
Puns
Qualities
Semantic fields
Similes
Skills

The session

1. First, ask the children if they know what a florist is. Floristry is the professional art of working with flowers. In groups, the children should note down instances when they might use a florist. No doubt they will suggest the more common occasions: weddings, funerals, birthdays, anniversaries and special dates such as Valentine's Day, Christmas and Mother's Day. You could perhaps turn this into a quiz to make it more exciting.

   Note: Show the children some 'wow' pictures of flower arrangements suitable for these events to get them interested and to help them visualise how wonderful and dramatic flower arrangements can be.

2. Show the children some other great pictures of more obscure times when a florist might be needed. These might include corporate events, awards ceremonies (like the Oscars), film and television sets, the fashion world (e.g. photo shoots, catwalks) and retail window displays.

   Tip: Look at the websites of McQueens, Rob Van Helden and Preston Bailey for examples of stunning arrangements for celebrity events. McQueens also does shop decoration for some of the big labels, as well as for the catwalk, and produces some great videos on YouTube which you could show instead of, or as well as, still images. LK Bennett and

   Mulberry have some lovely floral window displays, and for film and television production you could look at www.taylorcorps.com and www.livingprops.co.uk/floristry for some ideas.

3. Explain to the children that the idea of fashion extends into the world of floristry. Search the internet to find out what the latest trends are in floristry and which flowers are most popular at the moment.

4. Ask the children to describe their responses to the films and photographs. What particularly caught their eye? What did they like? Is it what they imagined floristry to be like? Could they see themselves doing something like this? Why/why not? Are they surprised by anything?

5. Tell the children that now they have seen the types of arrangements florists make, they are going to consider what skills, qualities and interests a successful florist must have. Working in groups, hand out a set of cards. Each card should have a skill, quality or interest written on it. The children must sift through the cards and divide them into three piles – skills, qualities or interests that are necessary, desirable or not essential.

Some skills, qualities and interests you might like to consider when creating your cards include: friendliness, imagination, being creative, standing up all day, coping with stress, working to deadlines, enjoying working with flowers, interpreting other people's ideas and needs, being a good listener, patience, enjoying practical work, working on your own initiative, teamwork, prepared for hard work and sometimes long hours (e.g. Christmas, Valentine's Day, Mother's Day), handling tools, using maths, dealing with the public, good time-keeping, knowledge of flowers and plant care, having an interest in flowers, art, design and business.

Also add some skills, qualities and interests that are not needed – for example, an interest in trains or the skill of rock climbing!

Variation: You could ask the children to separate skills from qualities and have a discussion about the differences between the two words. Ask the children to come up with their own definitions. You could discuss which is more important for a successful career, the skills, qualities or interests.

6   Discuss the children's decisions as a class. Why did they put certain skills, qualities and interests in particular piles? What skills, qualities or interests were the most unexpected?

7   Show the children photos of other jobs that involve flowers – for example, flower wholesaler, flower auctioneer, flower grower or picker, demonstrator, teacher or artist (Gregor

Lersch is a world leader and his work is fabulous). They could also work in the media as a writer, editor, photographer, author or publisher of books and magazines. Which job looks the most interesting?

8   Give the children some examples of flower magazines and books for them to have a look through. *Fusion Flowers, Fleur Creatif, Flower Arranger* and *Wedding Flowers and Accessories* show a very broad range of what can be achieved. As for books, there are lots out there, but my personal favourites include authors such as Jane Packer, Vic Brotherson and Moniek Vanden Berghe.

9   At this point, inform the children that they will now focus on the role of the writer for a flower magazine. To be successful in this area you must be able to have fun with language, and the way writers do this is by using techniques such as alliteration, rhymes, puns, semantic fields and adjectives.

10   Using copies of *Wedding Flowers and Accessories*, show children examples of the five techniques and make sure they understand what each one involves. Play some language games based around these techniques for reinforcement using their own names, what they like or flowers they are using.

11   In groups, the children then look through magazines to find examples of each of the language techniques. For example, each table could represent a specific technique and the children carousel around the room, adding to examples already found. Decrease the amount of time with each move.

Variation: Ask the groups to find examples of each technique, then one person from each group moves around the room, looking at what others have found and reporting back to their own group. The children should add their favourite finds to their own list. Tell them to hang on to these words and phrases as they might be useful later …

12 Inform the children that they are now going to make their own piece of fashionable floral jewellery, have their photo taken wearing it and then write a splash headline, a caption and a short, dynamic fifty-word paragraph about it (this is where their word stocks might come in useful). These can be used for display or on the school intranet.

Variation: The children could also create other commercial flower arrangements that they think would be attractive to customers.

Some things you might like to discuss

❀ Do you think you could be a florist? Why/why not?

❀ What might you like or dislike about the work?

❀ What skills have you learned today?

❀ What skills, qualities and interests do you have that are relevant to floristry?

❀ How might the skills, qualities and interests of a magazine writer differ to those of a florist? What will they have in common?

Learning to go: Encourage the children to use the internet to find out more about a career in floristry and ask them to produce a professional leaflet or web page that could be used by other students at their school. Some areas to find out about include: what training is needed, what different career paths are open to a florist (there are other opportunities available than working in a shop five or six days a week), what a florist might expect to earn, and expectations and pitfalls of the trade. They could go and interview a florist to find out what a typical week looks like – and perhaps get a day's work experience!

Extra English: Ask the children to write a set of instructions for a magazine explaining how to make the piece of flower jewellery featured in the photograph. Remember audience and purpose!

A fraction of maths: Many children are surprised at the important role maths has within floristry. Flowers bought from a wholesaler or market come in multiples of five, ten or twenty. Florists are advised to mark up the flowers by 100%. Often a customer will state an amount they want to spend, so the florist has to be aware of the cost per stem of each flower and foliage item and advise them accordingly. With this in mind, give the children the wholesale price of a bunch of flowers before VAT, tell them how many stems are in a bunch and then ask them to cost out the price of the arrangement they are about to make. Don't forget to include the price of any sundries (before VAT) and, giving the children a set price per hour, ask them to work out their labour costs and total everything up. How could they have made the arrangement cheaper? How much more expensive would it be if they added X, Y or Z?

Variations: Once the children have worked out sale price per stem, you could pose a series of conundrums – for example, a customer enters the shop and asks for a £20 bouquet. What flowers and foliage could they use? Add complications, such as the customer deciding they don't want a particular flower the children have selected. What would they substitute it with and how many would they use? Alternatively, the children could hold their own flower auction or cost out the price of their flower jewellery!

Chapter 9

Taking the blooming curriculum further

After using blooming curriculum in the classroom, you will no doubt want to take things a little further and look for other opportunities for using flowers in and around your school. To help you along, I have listed a few ideas that you might like to make a reality.

School flower show

Have your own school version of the Chelsea Flower Show! This is always an incredibly popular and successful event in schools where I have worked. Visitors love it and will want to talk to you and the children about the flowers and the work they have done. The children are full of rightful pride as they show friends, relatives and members of the local community their accomplishments, and visitors are rightly astounded by the children's work. It beats any parents' evening I've ever been to.

You can hold your school flower show at any time of the year. There are always beautiful, although very different, flowers, berries and foliage to choose from whatever the season. Why not have a flower show every term!

This could be a three-day special event that is intense and enjoyable. Children will get a taste of what it might be like to work in the floristry industry as they develop their knowledge, skills and understanding

in a range of subject areas, and all while working towards a wonderful final floral exhibition for parents and the community.

Include all the children in the preparations and operations – they will be working for a real purpose and audience and gaining invaluable skills and experience as a result. Remember the old adage: the more you put into something, the more you get out.

Spend two or three days creating a range of different flower arrangements with the children for the show.

Choose a light, open area to display the flowers and think about how you will use the space. For example, you could have displays against the walls, in the centre of the room or create themed areas for each arrangement.

Collect appropriate material or tablecloths to cover the display tables. Make decorative bunting to hang around the exhibition room – the bunting could show the children's favourite flowers or say something about how they enjoyed their blooming curriculum experience.

Put the arrangements into context and prepare display boards with associated work done by the children and photographs of the children at work. It's great for parents and visitors to see and read about the purpose behind the designs.

Write informative labels and headings for the arrangement stands.

Display teacher and pupil testimonials too: say what you enjoyed most, what you found the most challenging, what you would like to teach someone else, what you learned about yourself, what you have learned about flowers or the aspect of the curriculum you were covering – I could go on.

While you will need a formal letter to send out to parents, the children can design invitations, make posters and create web-based publicity for parents, guardians and the local community. You will get a big turnout – the more the merrier. You could even invite the press!

Create a 'I'm a Blooming Great Florist' certificate to hand out to the children who have participated in the flower show.

Produce a programme to distribute to visitors. Write a welcoming paragraph

and include information about who did what and why. Identify the flowers used and write a little bit about them too. Outline the timings of the day – one hour is usually sufficient to hold a flower show. Give visitors time to look around first (they will instinctively want to do this, so let it happen) followed up with a few words by the teacher or head teacher. You could get a few children to deliver a short presentation too, then hand out the certificates.

Set up a projector to show photos of the children in action during the show – children's faces while working with flowers are a real treat as they get so absorbed and engaged in the activity.

Consider if you want to sell products on the day too – for example, bunches of flowers, buttonholes made by the children or potted plants.

Offer refreshments: a bottle of squash, plastic cups and a couple of packets of biscuits don't cost much, but will make your flower show feel very warm and welcoming.

Provide a notebook for visitors to write their comments in about your flower show. This is always useful evidence when those government visitors come knocking.

Finally, take a photograph of each child with their arrangement before they take it home at the end of the flower show.

A transition project

A school flower show can act as a wonderful vehicle for a transition project. Over a six-week period in the summer term, teach the Year 6 children different floristry skills and produce arrangements for them to take home. The children could then put on their own transition themed flower show (you could use some ideas from the Change and Transition session in Chapter 8). Invite parents, staff and children from other year groups to come and take a look. The children could create bunting, and a personal timeline showing their favourite flowers, photos, words and drawings about themselves and their hopes for the future. In September, they could sow cut-flower seeds in the school garden ready for the next set of Year 6 students to use in the summer term. All this activity could be recorded in a personal dossier which they could take with them to secondary school as an example of work they are proud of at the end of their primary school career.

Project flowers

Create a six-week practical and imaginative cross-curricular scheme of work around the theme of flowers. Encourage children to chronicle their flower project in a film or school blog as they develop their knowledge, skills and understanding in a range of subject areas. You always have the option of finishing the project with a wonderful floral exhibition for parents and the local community. It represents deep learning with real purpose and audience – and inspectors will enjoy it too!

A flower a day keeps the inspector at bay

Without a doubt, flowers have an immediate positive impact on our happiness levels. They are psychologically proven to improve emotional health – people feel less depressed, anxious, stressed and agitated around flowers. When surrounded by flowers, people work more productively and demonstrate a higher sense of enjoyment and life satisfaction.

So, consider regularly decorating your school with flowers or handing out a bunch of flowers as a prize to the child or teacher of the week. Think how much nicer, brighter and happier your school could be.

Make your school inviting

Reception areas are the first places children, parents, visitors and inspectors see in your school, so show them that you care. Go further and regularly decorate classrooms, halls, offices and dining areas. See what a difference it makes.

Special events and celebrations

In preparation for those special events, annual celebrations or weekly assemblies, children can help decorate the school. For example, think about concerts, parents' evenings and open days.

Sports day

Make it professional and ask the children to create small bouquets to reward the winners and runners-up during your sports day. Remember the effect Jane Packer's bouquets had on the mighty Olympians at London 2012 – and you thought they were crying over their gold medals! Children will love it.

Staff training

Why not try a different approach to team-building exercises (who wants to endure an assault course, anyway) and have everyone get in touch with nature on a more gentle and artistic level instead? All the staff will go home with a beautiful arrangement at the end of the day. There will be no complaints as you treat your staff and start (or end) the term in an incredibly positive way. Flowers are far more motivating than banging drums, or heads.

Parent and child workshop

Make it a family affair and invite parents into the school to work on their own arrangement with their child. Flowers break down barriers, and this activity helps to develop relationships between schools and parents, schools and the local community, and parents with their own children. Parents may learn some new skills along the way and, as they work together, parents and children will be exploring all sorts of vocabulary.

Floristry club

Organise and run an after-school floristry club. Encourage children to take on different roles and responsibilities within the club. For example, they could help to decide how the club is run, agree agendas, fundraise or organise the annual end-of-year flower show. Another idea might be to join up with a local horticultural society and grow your own cut flowers.

Floral summer school

Make the most of the many beautiful flowers available in July and August, and offer the children and their families something really worthwhile to do over the long summer break.

Assemblies

Flowers can be a great stimulus for discussing many ideas in assemblies – just read Mick's introduction! Some schools have a thought for the week or focus on one composer's music for a week, so why not focus on one flower each week? This could be a flower of the season – from snowdrops to daffodils to dahlias. Equally, you could look at the more exotic flowers such as strelitzia or celosia.

Run your own school floristry business

Team up with your horticultural friends and grow your own cut flowers. You could use these to make arrangements and sell them to the public. How are you going to make your business viable? Perhaps you might consider donating flowers to a local old people's home.

Part 4

Useful things
to know

Techniques

Glue

Floristry glue is a must because it does not stain petals or foliage. For the glue to last, encourage the children to push the glue out gently from the end of the tube rather than squeezing the middle or near the nozzle. Amazingly, the less glue you use, the better the flowers will stick. The surfaces should be gently pressed together when the glue is tacky. It does not adhere straight away, but it does stick fast when it dries – this usually takes only a few minutes – but to some children this can seem like a lifetime!

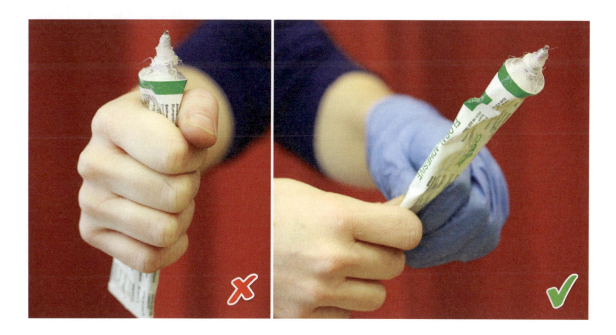

When gluing an orchid, dot glue around the back of the petals rather than the stem base. This will make it more secure.

Children will inevitably get glue on their hands. A good soapy hand-wash will get rid of most of it and whatever is left will dry and peel off easily. It is less easy to get off clothes, so I advise the wearing of aprons or an old shirt and, if you value your cleaner, lay out newspaper on the tables before you begin.

Glue dots are also available which are less messy but more expensive.

Wire

Using scissors for cutting wire

A good pair of floristry scissors will have a wire-cutting section towards the axle. Use this part of the scissors to cut any wire as using the middle or tapered end will damage the scissors.

Wiring

If you are right-handed hold down the end of the wire against the point where you want to start wiring with your left thumb (vice versa if you're left-handed) and, holding the wire reel in your right hand, begin wiring your arrangement.

Hold the reel in the palm of your hand with the wire feeding out between your index and middle finger. You can throw the reel over or through your frame and then grip the reel as described above and pull when you want to tighten the bind.

If you are using decorative wire, hold the wire between your thumb and index finger.

To finish wiring, simply cut with scissors and tuck in the end or twist it around another piece of wire.

Wiring pine cones and beech nuts

Most of the time you can get away with reel wire when wiring cones and nuts, but if the gauge is too thick you may need to purchase a fine 0.28 mm stub wire.

To wire a cone, cut a length of reel wire or stub wire and bend it lightly in the middle. Weave the wire around the base of the cone through the scales, twist the two ends together and attach to your arrangement. Trim and tuck in the ends.

To wire a beech nut, pass the lightly bended wire down the middle of the nut case and twist the two ends together under the base of the nut.

Floral foam

There are a range of floral foams available, some better than others. Oasis is a good, reliable make, but it is a little more expensive. You get what you pay for.

A good foam will not only soak up and hold a lot of water (some even contain flower food) but, importantly, it will not easily disintegrate. This can be crucial when you are inserting a large number of stems into the foam – and sometimes taking them out and putting them back in again! The latter will happen, although the more you can avoid it the better.

Soaking floral foam

To help flowers last for as long as possible, it is essential to soak the floral foam properly. This is how you do it. Fill a deep sink, bucket or bowl with water. Place the floral foam on top of the water and, in its own time, let it sink to the bottom. When it has sunk the foam is ready. Take it out and give it a gentle shake.

It is important that you do not force the foam down or run the tap over it. This will create air bubbles, which will inhibit the uptake of water and potentially damage the foam.

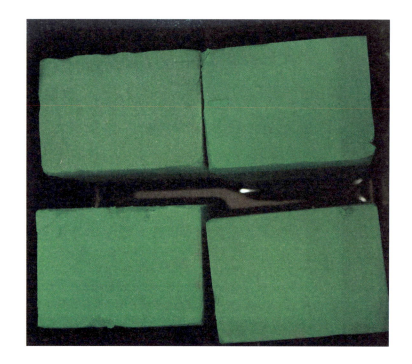

Cutting floral foam

Floral foam comes in all shapes and sizes, but in this book I have used rectangular block foam. You usually get twenty bricks in a box. You can cut it into thirds or halves, depending on your needs, and it is easy to cut with a sharp knife.

Wrapping foam in cellophane

This is a great and cheap way to create your own unique, water-proof container. Just think about how you wrap presents and you will have no problems.

Place your soaked foam in the centre of a piece of cellophane that has been cut to about twice the size of your foam. Then start wrapping. Raise two sides that share a corner, fold the corner flap to one of the sides and attach with sticky tape.

Continue using the same method around all the sides of the foam. You should end up with a wrapped brick with an exposed top.

Trim away the excess cellophane leaving about 1 cm above the top of the foam. This should stop any water overflowing when you water your arrangement. On that note, when watering your arrangement, do so gently and in small doses.

Cutting flowers

… for gluing

You want as little stem as possible so cut the stem close to the base of the flower. Try not to cut into the calyx or receptacle though as, if you do, the petals will fall away.

... to make more stems

Some flowers have flowering stems that branch away from the main stem – for example, spray chrysanthemums. You can cut these flowers in such a way that you can harvest more than one flower per stem, which can work out very economically when making arrangements.

There are two methods, each giving slightly different results. I generally use the following method as the flowers are more compact and therefore easier to place in the design for a specific effect. Cut the flowering offshoots as close to the main stem as possible, which will leave you with a long main stem.

Alternatively, you can cut the main stem at intervals, just above an offshoot stem.

... to insert into floral foam

Cut the stems at a 45 degree angle to aid insertion.

Some advice on inserting flowers into foam

Before cutting your stems, place your flower next to the arrangement to see how it looks, what height you want it and where you would like it to go. When you are happy, cut your stem at a 45 degree angle and insert it into the foam. Be careful not to cut off too much stem – you can always take away, but you can't add more.

Try to avoid inserting stems into the foam and then taking them out again. You will probably have to do this at some point, but the less you do it the better, otherwise you will end up with very holey foam. This will make inserting other flowers less secure and the foam may be more liable to disintegrate. This is another reason why it is wise to measure your flowers first.

Tools of the trade

Floristry scissors for cutting flower and foliage stems. You can buy some that also cut wire. I also use them to cut the material I use for containers.

Secateurs for cutting woody or thick stems.

Stem strippers for stripping leaves from flower stems. I only tend to use mine with roses.

Floristry glue for gluing your floral material without staining or burning the delicate flowers and foliage. I always use the cold glue in a tube made by Oasis.

Raffia is useful for tying posies and bouquets as well as for decorating your containers.

Reel wire is a strong, black wire used for binding materials together.

Bullion wire is a decorative wire that comes in many colours.

Magazines

I like all the magazines listed below for different reasons. If you get hold of copies, show the children as they love looking through them.

Fusion Flowers – flowers as high art and showcasing some of the most creative florists in the world. The focus is on photography and articles rather than 'how to …' Lots of inspirational ideas.

Fleur Creatif – a Belgium publication, available in English. This magazine is very similar to *Fusion Flowers* but focuses more on photography and 'how to …' features, listing the flowers used. There are very few articles. This is probably my favourite magazine of the lot.

Flower Arranger – a National Association of Flower Arrangement Societies (NAFAS) publication which looks at contemporary as well as traditional arrangement styles. *Flower Arranger* takes the essence of the above two magazines and distils and dilutes them into very manageable and cost-effective ideas. I like *Flower Arranger* a lot for this reason.

Wedding Flowers and Accessories – focuses on wedding arrangements (obviously), bouquets, buttonholes and table settings. I use this magazine for flower combination ideas, to look at colour, to show to children and for the text, as it is playful with language.

Websites

Design ideas

Fleur Creatif: www.fleurcreatif.com

Fusion Flowers: www.fusionflowers.com

Hans Flowers: www.hansflowers.co.uk

National Association of Flower Arrangement Societies: www.nafas.org.uk

Learning ideas

National Gallery: www.nationalgallery.org.uk

Plantlife: www.plantlife.org.uk

Royal Horticultural Society: www.rhs.org.uk

Science and Plants for Schools: www.saps.org.uk

Wild About Plants: www.wildaboutplants.org.uk

Thanks

First and foremost:

Scampi and chips in a Birmingham pub may not sound like the most auspicious of meals, but it was where the idea for the blooming curriculum was born and, therefore, I have a lot to thank it for. More specifically, I have a lot to thank Mick Waters for, the person who was sitting opposite me that evening, as he gave me the idea and encouragement to set up Blooming Curriculum. I have drawn on his deep well of knowledge, belief, good humour, support and kindness many times over the few years I have known him and during the writing of this book. He is one of life's amazing people and I'm fortunate to know him. Thank you, Mick.

Huge thanks also go to:

Caroline Lenton for her understanding and patience while putting the book together. There was a brief time when my mind was elsewhere and she was superb.

Jane Hewitt for doing a lovely job of the photos and helping me clean up at the end of the photo sessions.

Staff and students at the Arthur Terry School, Dearne Advanced Learning Centre, St Mary's Church of England Primary Academy and Nursery and Worsbrough Common Primary School. You were all terrific to work with and wonderfully hospitable.

Crown House Publishing for putting everything together and making the final product look amazing.

James and Sean Thomas at Wolverhampton Flowers and Brett Fitzpatrick at Jan Van Vliet, Birmingham, for sourcing flowers, offering advice and doing some great deals for me.

Last, but very definitely not least:

A huge thank you to Kevin for supporting me through this floral adventure. You are the kindest person I know. I really could not have done it without you.

Index

The flower arrangements   Let's learn about …   Curriculum subjects

Book a Blooming Curriculum Workshop

Listed below are some of the workshops which Julie can deliver in your school or organisation.

ONE DAY WONDER

A popular starting point with schools. The One Day Wonder session can be made up of anything between 1 to 5 workshops, each workshop catering for up to 30 students. This means up to 150 children in one day could be given the wonderful opportunity to experience working with flowers.

Each workshop includes:

- ☐ Ideas and activities linked to the national curriculum for teachers to pursue with the children afterwards.
- ☐ A 'Let's learn about ...' session.
- ☐ A demonstration.
- ☐ A practical session where the children create their own floral delight to take home with them.

THE SCHOOL FLOWER SHOW

This is a three day 'special event' that is intense and enjoyable. Children get a taste of what it might be like to work in the floristry industry as they develop their knowledge, skills and understanding in a range of subject areas whilst working towards a wonderful final floral exhibition for parents and the local community; a definite crowd pleaser.

PROJECT FLOWERS

Project Flowers runs for a half-term and includes weekly sessions for up to five weeks. Through the course of this project children will follow a practical and imaginative curriculum devised especially for the school. Children will be encouraged to chronicle Project Flowers in a film or school blog as they develop their knowledge, skills and understanding with flowers and in a range of subject areas. There is the option of finishing Project Flowers with a wonderful final floral exhibition for parents and the local community. Deep learning with real purpose ... and inspectors will enjoy it too!

Also available:

- ❀ Curriculum specific sessions
- ❀ Staff training
- ❀ Family workshops
- ❀ Summer school
- ❀ Floristry clubs
- ❀ Careers workshops

However, Blooming Curriculum is incredibly flexible and can be adapted to suit your needs, please get in touch for more information.

Visit bloomingcurriculum.com or email info@bloomingcurriculum.com

Have you ever tried teaching with flowers in your classroom?

If the answer is no, you have been missing out on an exciting and hands-on approach to the curriculum which captures children's imaginations and builds important skills and subject knowledge.

The challenge for teachers is to find imaginative ways to bring alive the subject matter prescribed in programmes of study. Julie Warburton has provided everything you need to get started; discover for yourself the transformative effects of teaching with flowers in this imaginative, thoughtful and beautiful book.

Stunningly illustrated, this book combines the intricate discipline of floristry with the wonder and opportunity of the classroom. The multi-sensory world of flowers is used as a living textbook to inspire and motivate children right across the curriculum.

Juno Hollyhock, Executive Director, Learning through Landscapes

This gloriously illustrated and clearly written book will do much to feed the souls of those many teachers who, after decades of almost exclusive emphasis on the functional and the measurable, yearn for fresh perspectives.

Dr Bill Gent, Associate Editor, *RE Today* magazine, Associate Fellow, Warwick Religions and Education Research Unit

As an enthusiastic botanist, I really hope that *Teaching with flowers* will help to raise the profile of the environmental, scientific and cultural value of plants; sowing the seeds of interest in the plant kingdom at an early age is a vital first step.

Dr Phil Gates, botanist and naturalist, @seymourdaily

Julie Warburton taught in an inner-city school, before moving on to school management. Through her work with the Black Country Challenge she has addressed the wider educational agenda as a teaching and learning consultant, working with a range of primary and secondary schools on transition and literacy. This book is the cross-pollination of her two passions: education and flowers. bloomingcurriculum.com

Teaching with flowers is a new addition to the 'Mick Waters introduces' series. Mick is perhaps best known as former Director of Curriculum at QCA (Qualifications and Curriculum Authority) and in this series of books he introduces a selection of the very best in practical resources for the curriculum.

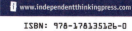
www.independentthinkingpress.com

ISBN: 978-178135126-0

9 781781 351260

Education